Qigong in Psychotherapy

You can do so much by doing so little

Qigong in Psychotherapy

You can do so much by doing so little

Patrick Dougherty, M.A., L.P.

WuWei Press

The information in this book is intended to be educational in nature and helpful in promoting wellness however it is not intended as medical care or medical advice or to replace the advice or services of a medical physician. Before undertaking any self-care regimens it is advisable to consult with one's physician, especially pertaining to healthcare needs that require medical diagnosis. The authors and publisher are not responsible for any adverse effects resulting from the application of information in this book.

Published by: WuWei Press, 2014.

ISBN-13: 978-0692313411

Printed in the United States of America

Book and Cover Design by Michelle Anderson – Grafik Distinction, Inc.

ACKNOWLEDGEMENTS

I wish to thank my readers for their generous help; Elizabeth Bernard for her eagle eye, and Bill Doherty and Susan Bougerie for their input on content and flow, as well as their never ceasing encouragement. I especially want to thank my editor Marian Sandmaier, gifted at her craft, whose numerous questions and suggestions helped to sharpen my writing. I also want to heartfully thank all my clients, whose identities are of course protected. Their daily courage to walk into the unknown, allowing me to go with them, is an ongoing inspiration. Finally, I am forever grateful to Master Chunyi Lin, who has inspired me through his teachings and actions, to live a more balanced and heart-centered life.

Table of Contents

INTRODUCTION

On a cold, windy December day in 1995, I sat in a Thai
restaurant in St. Paul, Minnesota with my friend Jim, an
African American man with whom I shared a passion for the
spiritual path. Once a year or so, we met to catch up and
compare notes about our inner journeys. At the time, I didn't
have much of one. I was one tired and stressed-out guy. I had a
fulltime psychotherapy practice, a busy teaching schedule, an
old home in perpetual need of repair, two active school-aged
children, and a marriage. Like almost everyone I knew, I was
doing too much with too little.

As Jim and I sat across from each other, enjoying our spicy food
on that freezing day, I asked him if he'd ever heard of a
mind/body practice called qigong (pronounced "chee gong").
All I knew was that it was an ancient Chinese system of
movement, breathing and visualization that supposedly was a
powerful stress-buster. I'd heard that if you practiced qigong
regularly, you were rewarded with renewed energy and a more
peaceful disposition. Smiling his wry smile, Jim replied that if I

was really interested in qigong, I should learn it from the source—a Chinese qigong master.

Returning my friend's wry smile, I asked: "Any chance you know where I might find one?" He said he sure did—in Coon Rapids, just 10 miles north of where we were sitting. There, he said, a Chinese man was teaching qigong classes at a community college.

I looked out the window at the snow, whipped into a white fury by the howling wind, and tried to take in the moment. Here I was on a cold day in Minnesota, eating a Thai lunch with my African-American friend, learning about a Chinese qigong master who was teaching just a short drive away. I didn't entirely understand why, but somehow the moment seemed propitious. "Give me the phone number," I said.

Four weeks later, I met Master Chunyi Lin and embarked on a journey that would profoundly change me, both personally and in the way I practice psychotherapy. In the pages that follow, I would like to share some of that journey with you. More importantly, I will offer you a path for enhancing your own vitality, emotional health, and capacity for joy via the simple practice of qigong. You don't need to become a Taoist or Buddhist; you don't need to study the breathing techniques of the yogis. You need only learn a set of simple tools for healing that will be available to you anytime, anywhere.

The Qigong-Psychotherapy Connection

There are plenty of books out there about Eastern mind-body practices, and some that focus specifically on qigong. And of course, there are numerous books about psychotherapy. My focus is integrative: this book offers a simple, powerful way to introduce qigong into Western psychotherapy and thereby maximize mind-body healing. Through 10 years of qigong practice, I have found that combining qigong tools with Western healing principles not only expedites the psychotherapeutic process but can also alter the outcome of therapy. Both in and out of therapy, the mingling of qigong practices with Western mental health practices can help you to enhance your energy, better meet life's daily challenges, and deepen your connections to the world around you.

Why isn't psychotherapy enough, all by itself? Let me say first that good therapy can be a potent tool to help people confront difficult, often lifelong struggles and guide them toward resolution. As a working psychologist for 30 years, I have the utmost respect for the power of the therapeutic process. But I often feel frustrated in not being able to help my clients translate the shifts they've made in therapy into more significant changes in their lives outside of my office. I am not alone in this regard; many therapists I have talked with share this frustration.

Too often, people get some therapeutic help—and in this age of managed care, maybe just barely enough help, and head right back into the world slightly better equipped to withstand life's stresses. Therapy often operates as a kind of psychological MASH unit, wherein we patch up people as best we can and then send them back into the chaos, hoping they will fare better. Integrating qigong into therapy offers immediate, effective tools to not only help people mitigate the effects of their stress-filled world, but to help them *maintain the changes* they have made in therapy.

I have also observed that psychotherapy can leave clients so self-aware that they consequently become unduly self-focused. This isn't a critique of certain schools of therapy, but rather of therapy in general—the kind I do included. This certainly isn't our intent as therapists, in fact, quite the contrary. But while our theories and tools teach us how to help our clients develop the *capacity* to be more meaningfully connected to the larger world, we frequently lack the tools and time to help our clients integrate this increased capacity for connection into reality. Too often, clients come away with more clarity about themselves, better communication skills and other relational strategies, but without actually deepening their connection to the world around them.

What I find most exciting about the integration of qigong into psychotherapy is its ability to help people open their "heart energy," thereby helping them to turn outward and deepen their relationships with others and the world around them. My experience as a psychologist—and as a human being—has shown me the happiest people are those who feel both cared about *and* care about others. This is the deepest potential of qigong—its capacity to help us to open our hearts, become more actively engaged with the world, and experience a sustaining sense of connection.

Who Can Benefit from This Book

The book addresses three audiences—psychotherapists, individuals who are in therapy, and all others who are committed to enhancing their emotional health and self-understanding and connection to the world around them. If you are a psychotherapist, you will learn a set of powerful, concrete tools to seamlessly integrate into your therapy practice. I highly recommend that you also practice these techniques yourself, both to enhance your own health and to deepen your therapeutic effectiveness. Regular practice will help you to be more calm, centered and open-hearted as you sit with your clients. Ram Dass once said, "You can only get as high as your therapist." I would amend that to, "You can only breathe as deeply as your therapist."

If you are currently in therapy, I invite you to use this book as a resource as you move through the healing process. You'll learn some simple techniques for changing negative thinking patterns, as well as ways to quickly calm yourself during challenging moments. The perspectives in this book may also help you clarify what you want to accomplish in your healing and growth process. Practicing qigong in tandem with your therapy work can not only help you resolve conflicts and enjoy life more, but also deepen your sense of belonging in the world.

For those of you who are not in therapy, this book will offer some simple ways to enrich your emotional life. You'll learn how the practice of qigong, in combination with key principles of Western mental health, can transform both your experience of yourself and your relationships with others. You'll learn how to use your breath and thoughts to increase your energy; how to use a couple of simple qigong movements to bring more calm into your life; and how to live with a more open heart.

Throughout this book, I will speak directly to the reader in plain, conversational language. I will avoid all psychological jargon (to the best of my ability). Where appropriate, I will share my own experiences with life challenges, my own therapy work, and my experience with qigong. While I am a therapist and a teacher of both therapy and qigong, I view myself first and foremost as a fellow seeker along the road of self-understanding. I invite you to join me on this road.

What is Qigong?

Qigong is a branch of Traditional Chinese Medicine (TCM), coming out of the Taoist tradition. The word "qigong" roughly translates as the practice of energy. The philosophy underlying this practice is that free-flowing energy throughout the body is vital to good physical and mental health. Many factors can block that energy flow, including stress, illness, and emotional conflicts. (TCM believes that unbalanced emotions are the *number one* cause of energy blocks, and then of the consequent physical and mental health problems.)[1] [2] Qigong, sometimes called "acupuncture without needles," is a simple method of movement, breathing, visualization and and sometimes sounds that can open up those blocks and restore you to your natural state of physical and emotional vitality.

Qigong was developed in China more than 5,000 years ago, as early Taoists searched for ways to live longer and healthier lives. They learned by studying what was in front of them—the natural world. They watched the turning of the seasons, the changes in weather, and how plants and animals responded to these shifts. As they studied nature, the Taoists noticed in particular the rhythms of the animal world. They saw that animals followed their instinctual natures, with no consciousness to distract them from their focus on staying alive and healthy. The Taoists watched and wondered: How was it that the heron could stand on one leg, poised to strike at a minnow, and calmly hold that position indefinitely? How could a mountain lion lie totally relaxed for an extended period, and then spring upon its prey in a lightning-quick, highly-focused explosion of energy? These animals, along with the rabbit, the monkey, the tiger, and others, taught the Taoists much about health, especially the natural and efficient use of energy.

The cultivation, harnessing, and optimal use of energy became a particular focus of the Taoists. They realized that human beings, too, could harness their energy and use it more wisely and efficiently. They identified rivers of energy running through our bodies, called meridians, which deeply influence our health and well-being. They witnessed how stress, unproductive emotions, poor health habits, and other factors could cause these meridians to flow sluggishly, or even become blocked. If one didn't readily address the blockage, physical and/or mental health problems often resulted, including headaches, back pain, stomach problems, depression, anxiety, and a general state of exhaustion.

But the Taoists didn't stop with diagnosis. They further discovered that if we listened to our body's elemental energies— rather than to our brains or emotions—we would find out how to restore our health and well-being. By tuning into the body's subtle rhythms, we would learn what to eat for maximal health, how to best adapt to the changing seasons, how to live healthfully in our particular environments, and how to heal ourselves when we were sick. The Taoists also developed many practices to help rebalance and restore the body's natural energy flow. These simple practices—repeated, refined, and taught over thousands of years—are at the heart of qigong.

Qigong is one of three components of Traditional Chinese Medicine, along with acupuncture and herbs. Qigong is sometimes used in conjunction with other TCM elements and at other times independently. Traditional Chinese Medicine views medicine and health very differently than we do in the West. When we think about using medicine, it's usually because we already have something wrong with us. We're feeling sick or in pain, and we hope that a pill or potion will make us feel better.

By contrast, TCM practices aspire too much more than "fixing" a medical symptom. Ken Cohen, perhaps the foremost Western scholar of Taoism and qigong, tells us that "…qigong differs from modern medicine in that it strengthens bodily resistance to disease, enhancing the function of the immune system, promoting intelligence, and prolonging life."[2] Cohen has further found that qigong can lower the body's stress response, alter entrenched traits such as Type A personality, and deepen what he calls "interpersonal sensitivity," the ability to be attuned and responsive to others' emotions.[3] In short, qigong is both preventative and deeply healing. It is medicine for the mind, body and soul.

Waking Up

When I started my own practice of qigong, I was an anxious, frazzled guy who drank too much coffee, ate too many sweets, and watched too much TV, all of which I thought I deserved as compensations for my daily stresses. I assumed that living under stress was a given—after all, most of my friends felt as harassed and hassled as I did. In other words, I felt like I was living a pretty normal existence. However, I hated feeling so chronically depleted of energy, and so powerless over my life.

I was also living on an emotional roller coaster. Having been in therapy a number of times, I believed that being "in touch with my feelings" at all times would help me to better understand myself. The idea was that close attention to my feelings would show me whether I was getting my needs met, and what I needed to do to feel better. Being Irish, of course, left me with a lot of feelings to keep track of and process. My therapists never warned me about the energetic impact of this self-absorbed state. Sometimes I felt calm and centered, but many other times I felt tuned up too high—like a screeching violin—or nearly reeling with exhaustion. I spent a lot of time trying to analyze these ups and downs as I hung onto the roller coaster by my fingernails. Something was seriously off kilter.

It wasn't that therapy didn't help me. It absolutely did. Working with skilled and compassionate therapists, I was able to break out of some very destructive patterns and to accept myself more fully. But therapy had also left me turned too far inward when I deeply needed to turn outward, toward other people and to the world at large. The happiness I sought remained elusive. My energy level continued to spiral up and down. I needed something more.

When I entered the classroom of our local community college for my first qigong class, I wasn't aware of what was missing from my life, or what I truly needed. I came to class to reduce my stress level, period. Looking toward the front of the room, I saw a slender, 30-something Chinese man sitting quietly. A few moments later, he stood and moved to the center of the room. "Hello, everyone, I am qigong master from China, Master Chunyi Lin," he began. "I know Americans feel funny about calling someone Master, so you can call me Chunyi, or Lin." Looking out at the class, he said, as his eyes crinkled at the corners, "Or, 'hey, Chinese guy.'"

And so began my first qigong class. Master Lin, founder of a school called Spring Forest Qigong, taught us seven simple body movements to help us focus our minds and balance our energy. He showed us breathing exercises and visualization practices. It was all surprisingly basic and user-friendly; even I got the hang of it pretty quickly. I liked Master Lin, whom I found to be humorous, down-to-earth, encouraging and admirably peaceful. Slowly, I began to feel pulled toward the practice of qigong.

At our teacher's suggestion, I committed to practicing qigong one half hour a day. At first, nothing seemed to change. But within a month, I began to notice that my sleep was better, and I was a bit less moody. After two months of daily practice, I was eating less junk food and drinking less coffee. I still watched too much TV, but I began to notice that it was depleting my energy rather than restoring it. I began to watch less. I got outdoors more, and slowly, very slowly, I began to feel an emerging sense of balance in my life.

Over the next several years, I continued to practice qigong. The benefits deepened. I found myself feeling more connected to others, less self absorbed. And yes, happier. Nonetheless, it took me a long time to begin to bring this simple practice into my work with therapy clients. As a clinician who did mostly long-term, psychodynamic and psychoanalytic-informed therapy, I was entrenched in these approaches and could see no opening for qigong as part of the healing process. Until I worked with Ron.

Breathing Lessons

Ron was a bright, articulate Protestant minister and a very motivated therapy client. But he was prone to intellectualizing his issues rather than experiencing them. Whenever he approached any emotionally-laden material, he would become physically agitated, but would quickly turn to analyzing his experience—the whys, the wherefores, the possible solutions. It was a learned response: Growing up, he and his older brother argued moral philosophy and religious theology with their college professor father, who admired intellectual prowess and disdained any show of emotion.

For awhile, I tried to "meet my client where he was" and reason with Ron, using my knowledge of psychological theory. But I was not his match in the debating department, and it really wasn't the issue. What was causing this man unhappiness and turmoil was being out of touch with his human experience.

One afternoon, I sat with Ron in my office as he got close to some emotional material and began to enact his usual routine of "stuckness": talking fast, with his voice a little higher-pitched than usual, and tilting forward in his chair, his body rigid with tension. I was doing what I usually did when I worked with Ron, groping around in my tool bag of therapeutic techniques and hoping for a way to help him move forward. I felt incompetent and frustrated—both with my client and with myself. Out of exasperation and an attempt to give myself some quiet time to ponder what to do next, I asked Ron to sit back in his chair and try some focused breathing—the kind of quiet, relaxed breathing I had learned in qigong.

We sat there for maybe three or four minutes, Ron breathing with his eyes closed while I hoped and prayed for some clarity to come to me about how to help him. Then, unexpectedly, he began to speak. "You know, I think I'm more lonely than I really ever knew. And I'm not really sure why."

But it wasn't his words, which coming from him was quite significant, as much as his body that I remember. As Ron spoke, his voice was noticeably lower and slower than before. His shoulders were no longer stiff and hunched, but relaxed and natural. Once or twice, I heard his voice thicken with emotion.

When I pointed out these changes a little later in the session, he nodded in agreement. "I can feel the difference, too," he said. "Somehow, I feel more *in* myself." This little shift opened the way for us to repeat this process every time he got stuck, often, though not always, with a similar outcome. The turning point—pausing to breathe—wasn't a particularly dramatic moment in itself. It was a small, quiet experience. But it was profound in the sense that it gave Ron a direct experience of connecting to himself, in a way that was both safe and liberating. That simple intervention became a cornerstone of my work with most clients, and I use it to this day. Particularly when I sense that clients need some kind of release, I ask them to simply pause and breathe.

After my experience with Ron, I began to integrate other tools from my qigong practice into my work with clients. I taught them a couple of basic movements, imagery techniques, and qigong concepts that helped them to ground themselves in their bodies and in the present moment. Because these practices are highly portable, I encouraged my clients to use them at home as well as during sessions. As I introduced qigong tools to clients, I continued to utilize traditional psychotherapeutic approaches. The results of this integration were surprising and heartening. For many clients, the pace of therapy accelerated. Others reported not only resolving long-standing problems, but also sensing a difference in how they greeted the world. They reported feeling more open, more connected. As one client put it, "I feel more heart-centered."

Building Bridges

Psychotherapists, therapy clients, and others interested in personal growth have long been frustrated by difficulty of sustaining emotional growth. How is it that we can bravely and persistently address our issues—dysfunctional marriages, neglectful parents, abuse, self-esteem problems, whatever else haunts us—yet so readily return to our old ways and outdated notions of ourselves? I have seen this backtracking happen thousands of times in my 30 years of practice. I have experienced it countless times in my own efforts to change and grow.

The good news is that many Western psychotherapists and physicians have begun to get seriously interested in the broader questions about how people heal. Why isn't the impact of psychotherapy more enduring? How does stress affect our psychological difficulties: is it a cause, an exacerbating factor, an impediment to healing, or all of the above? Is there a connection between our culture's epidemic of chronic illness and our emotional lives? Western scientists are now undertaking rigorous research on what Eastern healers have understood for centuries—the vital and complex connections between our emotions, our brains, and our bodily responses. Among other things, we're learning more about the powerful impact of stress on mental and physical health. We're becoming more open to mind/body approaches to healing—approaches that reap lasting benefits. My hope is that this book will contribute to this emerging healing paradigm.

A Brief Tour of the Book

The book is divided into three sections, each different not only in content, but also in length and style. The first section introduces the fundamentals of qigong—the basic concepts and techniques. The second section brings those specifics into therapy and daily life. The last section shows what can happen when we bring qigong and psychotherapy together in the big picture of life—how it can transform not only the process of therapy but also the ways in which people orient themselves in the world. Between the chapters, you will also find four exercises to help you begin to integrate the learning as you read.

Part One: Self-Cultivation. Self-cultivation is the process of understanding oneself, both mind and body, and learning how to live more consciously. The Taoists believe that it is necessary for individuals to cultivate themselves in order to authentically engage with others and with the larger world. This philosophy is consistent with what I believe good psychotherapy should have to offer, that working on oneself in therapy makes it possible to better engage with the world.

Chapter One presents the first task of self-cultivation—learning conscious breathing. I will show how focused breathing can help you achieve emotional balance and maintain a strong, enduring sense of well-being. Chapter Two highlights the impact of stress on our minds and bodies, and how simple it is to use qigong to intervene in our stress response. Chapter Three addresses the underutilized power of the mind. You will learn how to employ visualization and other kinds of imagery to deepen awareness and wisdom and improve your health and well-being.

Chapter Four focuses on energy. You will discover that everything—absolutely everything—is energy. Once you understand the nature of energy, you'll be able to make more informed decisions about every aspect of your life, from the work you do, to the music you play, to the friends you choose. The final chapter of Part One presents some foundational concepts of Taoist philosophy that offer a framework for the healing process. Throughout this section, I will show how these concepts and tools can be easily integrated with the best of Western psychotherapy.

Part Two: Healing the Self. People turn to therapy and other healing approaches because they are suffering. The hope is that seeking help from another will not only reduce your current suffering but also help you live a more happier life from this point forward. Integrating qigong into therapy can help this healing become more likely. Chapter Six is about bringing self-cultivation techniques into the therapeutic process. Through case examples, I will show how these simple concepts and techniques can impact the therapy process as well as be easily incorporated into daily life. Chapters Seven and Eight focus on the power of qigong practices to affect two common and challenging therapeutic issues, resistance to change and trauma, respectively.

Part Three: Beyond the Self. This section, just one chapter long, discusses the rewards of melding the therapeutic process with self-cultivation practice. These rewards include healing old wounds, helping you to better identify and meet your needs, improving your ability to communicate with others, raising your self-esteem and freeing up your flow of energy. But the deepest change—and the one that qigong most powerfully facilitates—

is the shifting of your consciousness to become more heart-centered.

This final chapter shows that when your heart energy opens, an incredible transformation takes place. You can no longer stay focused only on yourself. Instead, you find yourself drawn toward the goodness in others. You want not only to be loved, but also to love. You want not only to be known, but also to know others. You become aware of not only what you long for, but also the longings of others. The Taoist philosophy and the practice of qigong can show us the way to this place of deep and abiding connection.

I hope you enjoy the book and that it will help you to walk on this earth with more peace and joy in your heart.

Patrick Dougherty

November 2006

SECTION 1:
CULTIVATING THE SELF

CHAPTER 1:
THE POWER OF THE BREATH

Just yesterday, a client of mine was reflecting on how well she was doing in her relationship with her elderly mother. Carol had come to therapy in part to get help with her anger toward her ailing, bedridden mother, which made caring for her extremely trying. We'd spent maybe half a dozen sessions exploring the pain and hurt she'd suffered growing up with her mother, and the lingering resentment that complicated their current connection. As we sat together, I asked Carol what she thought was the most beneficial part of our work thus far. "Oh, that's easy," she replied. "It's the breathing."

Carol went on to say that when her mother's querulous demands really started driving her crazy, she would stop engaging with her mom, take an emotional step back, and begin some deep, slow, quiet breathing. As she breathed, she reminded herself of the times her mother had been good to her, and how aging and loneliness must be very frightening for her mother. "It helps me leave the old, angry daughter behind and come back to my current self," Carol told me. "When I can do that, it's so much easier to be with Mom—and even feel loving toward her."

As Carol stood up to leave the session and walked toward the door, she stopped for a moment and turned back toward me. "You know, that breathing stuff has helped me fall asleep a lot easier, too. I just love it."

Carol is not the only client who has benefited from this simple healing practice. Earlier this morning, I saw Elise, a married woman in her mid-forties. As soon as she sat down, she launched into a very long description of the way her heart had ached with loneliness while growing up, and how she was once again experiencing that ache in her marriage. I suggested that it might be more effective to use her heart, rather than verbiage, to tell me about her loneliness. I asked her to breathe quietly, allowing her breath to first sink into her body and then directly into her heart. For the next ten minutes, Elise sat wordlessly, tears rolling down her cheeks. Speaking from the experience of her sorrow as opposed to talking about it helped her to see more quickly what she needed to work through and what she needed to do in her marriage.

The Royal Road to Health

I was first introduced to the power of natural breathing in my own qigong practice. I quickly learned that breathing well significantly impacted the quality of my qigong practice. The deeper the breathing the more peaceful the practice. When I practice this natural breathing throughout my day some of that peace always came with it. Eventually, I started to bring breathing into my work with clients. From the beginning, I witnessed heartening and sometimes dramatic changes. By and large, my clients not only became calmer, but were also able to move into their feelings more quickly and deeply and then move out and beyond them. Stuck clients began to get unstuck. People began to more readily get to the real source of their pain—as well as to the source of their strengths. They became more centered, more self-loving, and more confident that they could do the necessary work to heal.

Few of us think of breathing as having an impact on health and healing. We tend to take our breath for granted and don't ascribe any particular benefits to it (except keeping us alive, perhaps!). Yet health care practitioners of the East have been treating emotional and physical health problems with breathing techniques for thousands of years. Sometimes, breathing is prescribed as an adjunct to other health care interventions; in other cases, it is used as a sole remedy, especially in cases of emotional problems or stress issues.

Qigong and other Eastern healing traditions rely on natural breathing not because they're primitive (which is what our Western ignorance has led us to believe) but because they have researched and practiced holistic health care techniques and seen the results. Over millenniums, they have witnessed that health, vitality, calm and self-awareness are enhanced by the practice of natural breathing.[1] The simplest thing you can do to enhance your health is to learn—or rather, relearn—to breathe naturally.

What is Natural Breathing?

If you want to know what natural breathing looks like, watch a baby sleeping. A baby takes deep, slow, even breaths. Their abdomen, sides and even their back around the lower spine expand with the inhale, and then the exhale is deep and complete. You can even sense the peace they feel at the end of the exhale. That experience is waiting for all of us once we learn, or relearn, to breathe naturally.

Stop here a moment and breathe the way you usually do. Count the number of breaths you take in the space of one minute. When you finish, read on.

How many breaths did you take? 10? 15? 18? You may be surprised to know that for optimum health, the ideal number of breaths per minute is 5 to 6. But few of us breathe that slowly. As we grow up, we start to breathe faster and more shallowly. There are many reasons for this, from social to familial. It is commonly believed that most Americans inhale only enough air to fill the top third of their lungs.

This is not good news because the most effective absorption of oxygen by the capillaries is in the bottom third of our lungs. To compensate for this insufficient oxygen absorption, the body instinctively takes more breaths. The average adult at rest takes 15-17 breaths per minute—fully three times the rate of optimal breathing.[2]

While the importance of healthy breathing has not yet reached the mainstream of Western medicine, our own science teaches that people who have lower blood pressure, a lower heart rate, healthy metabolism, a healthy immune system and less stress are likely to live longer than those that don't. Healthy breathing supports all of those bodily systems.

Little by little, the breathing practices of qigong and other Eastern traditions are beginning to infuse Western ideas about healthcare. Among the voices, and for many years' voices in the wilderness, are Herbert Benson, M.D., and Andrew Weil, M.D., who have been teaching and touting the benefits of breathing for over 25 years. Benson, who teaches at Harvard Medical School, helps people deal with anxiety by teaching them the "relaxation response." He asks them to relax, think of an object that brings them peace, and then breathe deeply and slowly. He has published numerous studies showing that this approach decreases anxiety, insomnia, headache, premenstrual symptoms, and a host of other health problems.[3]

Meanwhile, Dr. Weil has long taught breathing techniques to help address the rampant stress in our society. He believes that stress is either a cause or an aggravating factor in nearly all illnesses[4]—from back pain, to depression, to stomach problems. When people come to Dr. Weil for medical problems, he spends most of the appointment teaching stress reduction approaches, especially the practice of natural breathing. Often, he sits with patients and breathes along with them. (Can you imagine your own doctor doing that?) Dr. Weil says that of all the holistic approaches he teaches patients, he gets the most positive feedback about healthy breathing.[5]

Breathing: The Body's Natural Medicine

In my experience, you often don't need to learn a lot to know a lot—and this is especially true about the physiology of breathing. I will tell you enough in this section to help you understand why it's worthwhile to learn to breathe more efficiently and naturally. The bottom line—natural breathing supports every system in your body. Here are the basics:

Lungs. When we inhale, air enters our lungs carrying essential oxygen. Our lungs are lined with tiny capillaries that take oxygen out of the inhaled breath and send it into the bloodstream where all sorts of good things happen, of which I describe below. However, the exhale is as important because when we exhale, the lungs discharge carbon monoxide, a toxin that must be eliminated. Toxins leave our body via exhalation, sweating and bodily waste. Qigong practitioners and other Traditional Chinese Medicine healers believe that fully 70 percent of toxins leave via our exhale.[6]

Blood. The oxygenated blood travels through the body to do its wondrous deeds, such as helping to provide:

- Healthy functioning of all our organs

- Good digestion and absorption of nutrients

- Relaxed muscles in our extremities

- Efficient heart rate and lower blood pressure

Diaphragm. When we are breathing naturally and filling our lungs fully, the diaphragm (the muscle that holds the lungs in the upper part of our chest) stretches downward and consequently massages many of our vital organs, stimulating healthy blood flow. (This movement of the diaphragm explains why our abdomen expands during an inhale.)

Brain. Sufficiently oxygenated blood enhances the functioning of the brain and harmonizes the entire nervous system. You may be surprised to know that healthy breathing sometimes is recommended as a treatment approach for ADD because adequate oxygen in the blood to the brain can help it run more smoothly by helping balance the two sides of the brain.[7]

Immune system. When the systems described above are working efficiently and effectively, our immune system has all of the energy and resources it needs to do its job—stave off illness and infection.

Stress. When our bodily systems are working well, it is much easier for the body/mind to fend off stress. When our stress levels are low, we are less likely to be vulnerable to anxiety, depression and anger, as well as a host of physiological ills. (I will address stress in more detail in the next chapter.)

Do you want to bolster your immune system? Make natural breathing a habit. Do you have digestion problems? Take some deep, slow, quiet breaths several times a day. Is your brain a little sluggish toward the end of the day? Go ahead, try a few natural breaths. Stressed, anxious or depressed? Taking even one deep, healthy breath can immediately begin to mitigate those symptoms.[8] Obviously, natural breathing is not the only thing you need to do to maximize your health. But it is a vital—and simple—beginning.

Slow Down, You Breathe Too Fast

Not surprisingly, fast, shallow breathing has the opposite impact of slow, deep breathing. Following are some common body/mind consequences of shallow breathing:

- Not enough oxygen gets into the bloodstream
- Not enough toxins leave the body
- Our organs function less effectively
- Our digestion and absorption of food is less effective
- The brain struggles with clarity and continuity

- The heart has to work harder to do its job, raising blood pressure and sometimes heart rate
- Our extremities can become tense more easily
- Our immune system works less effectively
- We become more vulnerable to the stresses of life, which in turn makes us more vulnerable to anxiety, depression, anger, and other energy-draining emotional states

So Why Don't We Breathe Easy?

In an ideal world, I would ask you to practice healthy breathing for 10 minutes right now so you could begin to feel the benefits of it and then trust that you'd never want to take a shallow breath again! But I am a psychologist, and a very human human myself. So I know that imparting information alone isn't enough. Many of us need to understand why we aren't breathing in our own best interests.

For most of us, two obstacles get in the way of better breathing. The first is habit—we're simply used to breathing quickly and shallowly. If that's the main issue for you, you'll learn practices in this book that will help you to form new, healthier breathing habits.

The second, more challenging obstacle, is our resistance to inhabiting the life and emotions that our breath takes us into. To illustrate this point, let me tell you about a client of mine. A couple of years ago, I was working with a woman in her mid-30s named Lauren. One morning, she came into my office as usual—late, flustered, and already talking. While still taking off her coat, she described to me all the things she'd already done that morning as a way of explaining her tardiness. "I dropped off the dog at the groomer's, and then had to pick up the cake for my uncles' birthday party tonight, and then ran over to the gym for my morning workout—and that was all after getting the kids off to school!" Barely taking a breath, Lauren plopped onto the couch and continued talking a mile a minute about the struggles that had brought her into therapy.

For a moment, I sat silently across from her, sinking into my own breath and my body. As I did so, I had a clear sense that this woman wasn't really in my office yet. So I gently asked Lauren to stop her narrative and just sit quietly on the couch for a few minutes. "Just breathe, slowly and deeply," I suggested. "Take some time to sink down and connect with your body." Lauren took about five breaths and then burst into tears. A few moments later, she choked out between sobs, "I hate my life."

What had just happened? When Lauren used her breath and consciousness to sink into her self, she immediately got in touch with a part of her that her shallow breathing and breakneck schedule had allowed her to avoid. It was the part of her that felt empty, tense and miserable. It was a turning point in our therapy work. From this point on, Lauren began to focus on what she truly yearned for—connection and serenity—and to slowly bring these qualities into her life.

For many of us, shallow breathing serves a similar purpose— blocking us from knowing who we truly are. Dennis Lewis, author of *Free Your Breath, Free Your Life*, puts it well, "The major goal of shallow breathing is the unconscious buffering of our experience of self." [9] It can be painful to face our own sadness, aloneness, or anger. Yet, as Lauren discovered, directly experiencing the self is the first step toward healing.

SIMPLY BREATHING

I'm going to teach you a breathing exercise from the qigong
tradition that is both simple and very powerful. But before we
get started, let me make a few preliminary suggestions:

Practice often. The more you practice healthy breathing, the
more it will become part of your life. Once you do this exercise
a few times, you'll be able to practice it anywhere: while driving
your car, standing in line at the grocery store, or lying in bed.
By learning this very simple technique and committing it to
memory, **you're starting on a path that will benefit you for the
rest of your life.**

Don't work hard at it. This is central to the qigong approach
to breathing—and one of the reasons I love it. You should not
strain to change your breathing. As Stewart Olson in the Jade
Emperor's Mind Seal Classic suggests, "Picture your mind as a
dirty glass of water. The more you agitate it, the cloudier it
becomes. However, if you just let the glass sit, the debris will
gradually filter to the bottom and the water will become clear
again. [Trying] to make the breath deep, slow and harmonious is
like stirring the water; the breath cannot be natural because you

are forcing it. But by just letting it go, it will sink of its own accord and become natural."[1]

Trust your intention. A genuine desire to breathe healthfully will go a long way. My teacher, Master Lin, likes to say that when you practice any qigong exercise, you can only do it "good, better, or best." So just put honest effort into this breathing practice, and forget about perfection. I know this is difficult for most of us who were raised in the West, but give it a try!

Exercise 1: The Conscious Breath

This first breathing exercise is very easy to learn, but don't be misled by its simplicity. If you practice it regularly, it can have a profound and enduring impact on your mental and physical health.

To get started it is best to choose a quiet, comfortable place at a time when you will not be interrupted. Or, just do it where you are. Remember, good, better and best. It is a very simple exercise. You can either sit or lie down; the important thing is to try to keep your spine straight. Close your eyes and take a few quiet breaths until you feel relaxed. Then simply observe your breath. That's it. Just watch your breath go in and out.

Qigong teachers do not tell their students what to expect from any exercise because they want them to experience it fully, free of preconceptions. Let's honor that tradition here. Before reading the next paragraph, do the above exercise for five minutes. Once you've finished the exercise, read on.

What were you aware of on the physical level during this brief practice? You may have noticed some changes in your body. For example, you may have become aware of the difference in air temperature when you breathed in versus when you breathed out. Or you might have noticed that one particular nostril predominated in the breathing process. Did your chest or abdomen expand? Maybe you felt some physical sensations, maybe not. Or maybe you were aware of nothing more than the air going in and going out.

While doing this exercise, many people notice for the first time how shallow their habitual breathing is. Many of us are a bit taken aback by this recognition, for we tend to simply assume that we breathe deeply. But developing awareness of your customary breathing pattern is a good thing because it will encourage you to pay more attention to your breath. If you stay with this exercise long enough—just attending to your breath without trying to change anything—you will tend to naturally slow down and deepen your breathing.

If you're like most people, you may also have noticed a lot of thoughts running through your head as you did this exercise. Or perhaps you were aware of certain emotions. That's fine. Don't expend a lot of energy trying to change or suppress your experience. Instead, when you become aware of thoughts or emotions during this process, just notice them, gently let them go, and refocus on your breathing. You may need to do this refocusing many times during your practice, especially at first. It's natural and to be expected.

Conscious breathing not only leads to healthier breathing habits, but also is in itself transformational. As Dennis Lewis observes, "Conscious breathing helps us to cultivate inner stillness and presence. It also helps us to be present to ourselves without judgment and analysis."[2] Imagine, for a moment, experiencing yourself whole, with no need to improve, squelch, "grow up," or otherwise change yourself. Herein, perhaps, lies the breath's deepest potential for healing—its capacity to gently, lovingly restore us to ourselves.

CHAPTER 2:
STRESS: THE HIDDEN SABOTEUR

Who tiptoes doesn't stand,
Who strides doesn't walk....[1]
— Tao Te Ching, Verse 24

For years, I marveled at couples who worked hard on their issues
and truly wanted a better relationship, but would then explode
into blame-slinging fights as though they'd never spent an hour
in therapy. Or the middle-aged father who'd spent years
working on his anger—the pain of its origins, the remorse at its
consequences, the alternative responses—and then found
himself shrieking in rage at his teenage daughter over a small
matter. Or the painfully shy woman who worked hard in
therapy to address her fear of interacting with others, but was
unable to take out of my office anything she'd learned inside.
Only recently have I begun to recognize the source of this

powerful, relentless sabotage. It is something we think we know all about, yet seem helpless to contain. It is the stress response.

In the psychotherapy profession, we usually give little more than lip service to the role of stress in contributing to the problems that bring clients into our offices. We pay even less attention to the ways that stress interferes with successful treatment, even when clients work long and hard on their issues. The truth is, we psychotherapists don't understand stress much better than the average person. We throw the term "stress" around as though it is merely a lens to help us understand our clients' lives. We acknowledge it—"yes, yes, of course, stress is involved"—then move swiftly on to the "deeper" issues.

When we do recognize the power of stress, it is usually in extreme situations. When a couple is considering divorce, when an individual is suffering a major loss, or when a family is struggling with alcoholism. Here, we recognize that they may be anxious, short-tempered, depressed, and prone to poor decision-making because of the stress of their particular crisis. But what of the less dramatic, repetitive pressures of everyday life—the hectic work schedules, the chaotic family lives, the chronically tense relationships, the unsatisfying jobs? This "ordinary stress" wreaks quiet havoc on our bodies, minds, and spirits. What makes this kind of stress particularly insidious is that it is largely hidden and unacknowledged. Because we accept our daily pressures and hassles as "normal," we rarely appreciate how powerfully they can undermine our ability to get ourselves back on track.

The Forgotten Body

Several years ago, a former client named John called to say he needed to see me as soon as possible. John had endured a very tough childhood. The older of two boys, he'd grown up with an alcoholic mother and a mostly absent father. One dynamic we'd worked on in therapy was how, growing up, his mother was kind and attentive (when sober) to his brother, cousins, and friends, while pointedly ignoring John. This had left him very hurt, bitter, and acutely vulnerable in adulthood to his wife's expressions of warmth and caring toward others. John had worked hard on these issues in therapy, confronting his anger and grief about his mother, getting involved in Adult Children of Alcoholics and talking honestly with his wife about his sensitivity. By the time he'd left therapy, he felt he had pretty well resolved this deeply painful part of his past. He was ready to embrace his life.

When John came in to see me, it was a beautiful spring afternoon. My office window was open, the air was fresh, the birds were singing. The world seemed sweet and full of hope. Then John strode into my office like an emissary from another world. His body was rigid, his face tight with misery. As he sat down heavily on the chair across from me, he stared down at the carpet, avoiding eye contact. All in all, he seemed more like the guy who had first walked in my office several years ago than the man who had terminated therapy several months earlier, full of hope and renewed energy.

"It's my wife," he muttered. His wife, Sherry, a college professor, had always been a loving wife; he'd never had reason to doubt her devotion or fidelity. But in recent weeks, he'd found himself obsessed with jealousy. Sherry was planning to have dinner with

Eric, a teaching colleague whom she'd known for over 20 years. From their earliest years as college professors, they had annually marked the end of the academic year with a celebratory dinner. John knew both Eric and his wife, and it was clear that their relationship was strong and affectionate. He had no reason to believe that Eric and Sherry were anything but good friends.

Yet John found himself acutely jealous of Eric and furious with Sherry. As he told me the story, I could hear the suffering in his hoarse, dispirited voice. John told me he felt "crazy inside," not just with jealousy and anger but because he knew that his feelings were absolutely unwarranted. "I just can't stop myself," he said.

As I listened to John, I was perplexed. I wracked my psychologist's brain for something I might have missed in our earlier work, some piece of unfinished business, or some new insight into this old dilemma. Earlier in my career, I would have painstakingly deconstructed the conflict with my client, identified the hot button, and done more therapy work around that specific issue. But my recent qigong training got me listening to John in a different way. I saw and sensed his shallow breathing, his tense muscles. Something told me that his body, not his psychology, was driving this issue.

After John finished his story, I told him I had learned a few things since I'd last seen him. "Would you be willing to try something new?" I asked. He breathed a sigh of relief. "You bet," he said.

I'll come back to John a little later.

Inner Alarm Bells

Let do a quick review of Physiology 101. Each of us has an autonomic nervous system, one that we normally don't think about or believe we can do much to control. It is a regulatory structure that helps our body adapt to its immediate environment. This system has two parts, the sympathetic nervous system (SNS) and the parasympathetic nervous system (PNS). The PNS helps the body to run smoothly and carry out its normal life tasks. It helps regulate our digestion, blood pressure, heart rate, a healthy blood flow to the brain, and our immune system, to name just a few of the things it does. It helps the body run smoothly and it saves energy. Most of the time, this system is quietly in charge of the body.

But sometimes, the SNS takes over. The activation of the SNS is the stress response, better known as the "fight or flight" response. (Recently, the stress response has been expanded to include the "freeze" reaction as well.) This system helps our body protect itself when it is threatened. We don't need to think about it: our lower, or "reptilian," brain simply kick-starts the system. Our heart rate and blood pressure pick up; our metabolism increases, and more blood flows to our extremities. Simultaneously, the SNS suppresses blood flow to the brain and other organs, and curtails the effectiveness of the immune system. We become more aware and vigilant as our strength increases, our reactions quicken, and our breathing becomes shallower. Our body focuses on survival.

Why do all of these changes take place? A good analogy is that of a zebra being stalked by a lion. When the zebra is eating her breakfast grass and suddenly sees a lion poised to strike, she doesn't ponder a response. Instinct kicks in, along with the

SNS. The zebra's heart rate increases and other necessary systems ratchet up to maximum capacity. There's no need for her to digest her already-eaten portion of breakfast, given that she soon may become someone else's. The zebra's immune system slows down—why worry about a virus that will spell trouble tomorrow if there might not be a tomorrow? No need to use the whole brain, just the part that helps us focus on the immediate threat. As for breathing, the zebra will use just enough to keep her system running, the body is running at maximize efficiency (For a very engaging and detailed exploration of the physiology of stress, see *Why Zebra's Don't Get Ulcers*, by R. Sapolosky.)[2]

Just like the zebra, we come equipped with an innate alarm system. Whenever we feel threatened, our lower brain acts instinctively to turn on our SNS. The difference is that we humans have thinking brains as well as survival brains. In human beings, what's supposed to happen next is that the thinking center of our brain kicks in and makes a key judgment—should the stress response be allowed to continue, or should it be switched off? But this judgment call takes place only if the higher brain is conscious that the SNS has been turned on in the first place, and if the higher brain can tell whether the threat is real.

This is where we often get into trouble. Our forefathers and foremothers, in their long trek through evolution, certainly faced many immediate threats to their survival, from saber-toothed tigers to fierce battles over scarce food. By contrast, in today's Western world relatively few of us face life-jeopardizing situations. But our bodies no longer know what is a genuine threat and what is not. <u>The stress response turns on—and often</u>

stays on—in situations where our well being is not truly threatened.

The Hazards of Stress

How many of us really believe that getting stuck in a traffic jam, which in turn will get us to our kid's soccer game a bit late, is truly a threat to our survival? Our thinking brains understand that it's not. But do our survival brains? Often, mine doesn't seem to. I've often rushed to my own child's game, furious at other, slower drivers and feeling my heart knocking in my chest as though I'm preparing to fight for my life. It doesn't occur to me that there is anything wrong with me either. I know many parents feel this same stress at being late to games.

The problem is that this "ordinary stress" can wreak serious damage. Many of us are familiar with the anxiety, irritability, fatigue, and desire to withdraw from others that can accompany daily stress. We know the "feelings" of stress, but we're less aware of its long-term effects. Ken Cohen, the noted Chinese scholar and qigong teacher, tells us what chronic stress does to our "qi," or flow of energy:

> Stress causes a general state of physical and mental tension, a condition that the Chinese call "wai qiang nei gan"—"the outside strong, the inside rots." When we can't easily change our circumstances, we often internalize our frustrations in muscular tension. Beneath this hard shell, the qi becomes sluggish, unable to flow smoothly, either internally or between the body and the environment.[3]

The outside strong, the inside rots. How many of us realize, that as we clench our car's steering wheel, or yell at a family member, or toil until midnight over a deadline, that our insides are rotting? As Cohen notes, part of that deterioration is internal, both physical and psychological. Chronic stress is known to contribute to heart disease, gastrointestinal problems, headaches, muscle tension, sleep problems, weight gain, and reproductive problems for both men and women. There is also some evidence that stress contributes to cancer and osteoporosis. At an emotional and psychological level, stress has been linked with depression, anxiety, and as most of us know, it also leaves us irritable, tired and feeling sorry for ourselves.

The effects of chronic stress are not only internal. As Cohen notes, stress also undermines our ability to interact with our external environment—especially with other people. How many of us take into account that when we're stressed, we're unable to respond well to our spouses, partners, children, friends, and officemates? Not only does our stress often hurt these relationships, but what these relationships have to offer us to help mitigate our stress is frustratingly out of reach too.

John: Going Deeper

Back in my office, I spent a few minutes educating John on natural breathing and relaxation and its benefits to body and mind. He responded that both deep breathing and feeling relaxed were very hard for him. From our previous work together, I knew that to be true. I also realized that I had totally overlooked the likely impact of his difficulty in relaxing, especially once he'd left the support of weekly therapy sessions. I told John that with some patience and guidance, everyone could learn to become a little more relaxed. He said he was ready to give it a try.

I guided John through a basic relaxation exercise, asking him to close his eyes, breathe naturally, and then progressively relax each part of his body, starting with his feet and legs and continuing with his lower torso, abdomen, lower back, and so on, all the way up to his face and scalp. After about five minutes, when he seemed relatively relaxed, I asked him to visualize his wife, Sherry, sitting in front of him. I then asked him to say out loud what he wanted to say to her. "What is it that you really want her to know?" I asked. He sat silently for three or four minutes, until a single tear slid down his cheek. Softly and sadly, he said, "I miss you."

When John opened his eyes, he told me that in the quiet place his breathing had taken him into, he realized that he could not remember the last time he and Sherry had spent any intimate time together. They'd been so caught up in their jobs, their kids' activities and the general needs of the household—they'd lost touch with each other. He realized then that he wasn't jealous of Eric, per se, but of the time his wife was going to spend one-on-one with someone else. Time together was what John most wanted from Sherry.

As we continued to talk, John began to recognize how stressed out he'd become both at work and at home, and how chronically exhausted and irritable he was. He saw how remaining unaware of his need for connection with Sherry caused him to approach the issue of "the dinner" with anger and accusation, which had only increased the distance between them and had worsened his stress. Shaking his head at his folly, John thanked me and said he now knew what he needed to do—ask his wife for a date. As he left, he said, laughingly, "You shouldn't teach your clients to breathe too early in therapy, or your office might empty out."

Clearly, John's sympathetic nervous system had been working overtime in response to the perceived threat of his wife giving attention to someone else. Between the hair-trigger responses of his reptilian brain and his particular childhood history, John felt powerless to mitigate its effects—even though his cognitive mind knew that his obsessive jealousy was way off base. At one point, he said it felt as though he were trapped in a speeding car without a steering wheel; a car that perpetually returned to the same unfolding scene of Sherry and Eric enjoying an intimate dinner. Try as he would, John couldn't seem to do anything to stop the car or shift the scenario.

Looking Within

Our mind has many wonderful functions, and one of them is helping us to make sense of the world we experience. If you hear a loud bang coming from a block away, your mind might conclude something like "fire-cracker" or "car backfiring." Likewise, if you hit your thumb with a hammer, taste a jalapeño pepper, or see a hummingbird flit by, your mind will come to a conclusion about those experiences. Most of the time this mental function is very useful, helping us to learn from our experiences and create meaning from them.

But when we suffer from stress—especially chronic stress—this process can go haywire. The mind will always strive to find some reason to explain our irritable mood, our depression, or our impulsive behavior, and it will usually come up with a cause other than the personal choices we are making. I have witnessed this process countless times in individual and couples therapy. When someone is suffering the symptoms of chronic stress, they typically blame their distress on something outside themselves—their impossible job, their rush-hour commute, their unruly kids, or their insensitive spouse. Usually, they collect enough evidence to make the case in their mind and sometimes even in mine. These scenarios always have some merit, of course; they wouldn't have the power to convince unless some evidence exists to build the case. <u>But the mind is fully capable of **distorting** facts to help it make sense of the body's experience—especially the experience of stress.</u>

This point is critical for people in relationship struggles. If your life is generally very stressful, and if you're also experiencing at lot of stress in an important relationship, your perceptions of that relationship <u>will be questionable</u>. Even in the best of times, none of us likes to admit that we are part of the problem. But when you are stressed, your mind is fuzzier and less trustworthy than usual. The more severe and long-lasting the stress, the more befuddled your mind is apt to be. As your confused brain struggles to come up with an explanation for your distress, it will more than likely decide that the other person in the relationship is more to blame—evidence be damned!

The Legacy of Childhood

In John's case, his difficult childhood also played a part in his hair-trigger response stress. When you grow up in a chaotic family like his, you're likely to enter adulthood with a heightened sensitivity to stressful situations—especially ones that remind you of your childhood pain. In therapy, John achieved a lot of the mental and emotional clarity he needed to resolve his early distress; however, something was missing from our therapy work: attention to the *physiological* legacy of stress.

Given John's history, his stress response would easily be triggered regardless of all of the cognitive and emotional work we'd done. Recall that the stress response, programmed to ensure our survival, kicks in faster than our thinking brains do. Once sensitized, the stress response will continue to be readily triggered, leading to faulty thinking and decision-making about our current situation. <u>To slow down the body, we must enlist the body</u>, which was why I taught John relaxation techniques as an antidote to his stress response. I had missed this in our early work together.

For people like John, it is especially important to help them with their stress response in therapy. Research shows that the impact of chronic childhood stress can be lifelong and severe. Studies by the National Institute of Child Health and Human Development suggest that chronic exposure to any stress in childhood can permanently alter the stress response, rendering it extremely sensitive to later stress and paving the way for serious, life-threatening disease.[4] John's hypersensitivity to his wife's behavior is an example of the kind of extreme vulnerability that can result from chronic childhood stress.

Due to the way we're wired, we need not have suffered a genuine threat to life or health during childhood to develop a hypersensitive stress response. Any kind of chronic childhood stress will do. Imagine a man who grew up with a mother who glared at him coldly and condescendingly whenever she objected to his behavior. Guess what happens to this man's physiology whenever his wife casts a disapproving look his way? Or imagine a woman whose father controlled the family by frequent anger and yelling. Guess what happens to her body whenever her husband begins to elevate his voice in irritation at her? Certainly, it would be helpful for these two to sort out the emotional turmoil of growing up as they did. But, if they aren't also helped to intervene in their habitual bodily responses to these events, they will continue to react with fear, anger, muddled decision-making, and heightened vulnerability to illness. Despite their best efforts, talk-centered psychotherapists and their clients are frequently thwarted because, too often, physiology trumps.

Qigong and Stress: Let Your Body Be Your Guide

People often come to our qigong classes because they are in physical or emotional pain and are desperately seeking relief. Stress is often an underlying issue and most class participants know that. Either the offerings of conventional medicine aren't working, or students are seeking an alternative approach because they are not comfortable with the side effects or other aspects of modern medicine. Whatever their reason for trying qigong, most people hope that it will give them relief from their symptoms—quickly.

It is an understandable hope. However, while qigong is a powerful approach to healing many health problems, symptom reduction is usually not immediate. There are two reasons for this. First, these health conditions have usually developed over a long period of time, and a gentle, natural healing approach such as qigong cannot be expected to reverse those conditions overnight. Secondly, because long-standing, stress-induced problems (the kind that most people bring into qigong class) are present within the entire bodily system, the body doesn't simply have an acute problem, but a systemic problem. Since your body understands the problem this way, it will use the energy you cultivate as it sees fit. Your mind cannot dictate the benefits your qigong practice; your body decides. Fortunately, the body is a trustworthy healer.

Let's say you're suffering from a stress-related stomach problem. While you may long for nothing more than a pain-free gut, your body instinctively knows that if it treats the stomach first, your relief will be temporary. That's because you cannot support a healthy, balanced energy in the stomach area when your overall system is out of balance. So, a qigong practice will first attend to the foundation of your health, and then attend to the specifics. Master Lin often tells us, "You would not fix up a nice bedroom on the second floor of a house if you knew the foundation was crumbling."

I liken this situation to a client coming into therapy to work on his "anger problem" while continuing to live a very stressful life, filled with long work days and little downtime. He sees his problem as anger, and he simply wants it to stop causing himself, and others, unhappiness. He knows that he lives under a great deal of stress, but he believes it to be normal and unavoidable. "That's just life!" he says. Now, we could approach his anger through a myriad of therapeutic approaches, but if he continues to live the way he is living—in a state of chronic exhaustion and allowing no time for himself—how far are we likely to get with his anger problem?

This doesn't mean that addressing stress is a quick and easy antidote. I usually address stress early on in therapy, but more often than not, after I share this piece of enlightenment, my clients initially do little to change their lives. But sometimes, later on, when they get stuck, I will remind them of the way that stress may contributing to their ongoing struggles. When they see the painful consequences in the here and now, clients will often begin to feel more responsible for their problems and more willing to make the difficult choices that will reduce their life stress.

Changing the Unchangeable

While physiology often wins the day, does it follow that this heightened sensitivity to stress is necessarily a permanent legacy? Traditional Chinese Medicine doesn't think so. Unlike Western medicine, TCM views the body and health in a state of constant change, just as everything in nature shifts and evolves. Nothing is permanent; everything one way or another is treatable. So, if you were diagnosed with stress hypersensitivity due to chronic exposure to childhood stress, a daily practice of simple qigong movements, along with focused breathing and the use of calming imagery, might be recommended to rebalance your body's energy. TCM believes—as do I—that this practice would have great potential to alter your "permanent" condition, restoring you to a state of free-flowing energy, health, and well-being.

A few years ago I worked with Burt, who was 72 and long retired. He was suffering from depression, in large part because of the growing neuropathy in the legs, a numbness that was slowly progressing upward through his calves. Because he was a gregarious man who had many family commitments and a very active social life, he found his growing disability very stressful. He wanted relief from his depression and to have a place to talk about his fear and grief around the neuropathy.

I referred him to a qigong class, as well as used qigong techniques and principles in our therapy sessions. Burt discovered that he loved qigong. In class, he made several new friends (he couldn't help himself) and after a few months of therapy and a regular qigong practice, not only had his depression disappeared, but also his neuropathy was receding. (His doctor told him that whatever "funny Chinese thing" he was doing was obviously having an effect because the receding neuropathy was not due to any Western medicine treatment.) Burt had slowed down his social schedule a bit, too, as he had learned to listen to his body's energy rather than only to his enthusiasm for socializing. He was a little disappointed to have to stay home a bit more, but, as he acknowledged, he was feeling both healthier and happier. Laughing, he added, "Thanks for teaching me that funny Chinese thing!"

The Courage to Feel

Unfortunately, it's not as easy for everyone as it was for Burt to get on a healthier path. Taking the first steps toward liberation from stress can require great courage on the part of the client— as well as plenty of awareness on the part of the therapist. A few years ago, a 44-year-old woman named Kathy came in to see me. She had plenty of issues to deal with: a newly empty nest, as her youngest child had just left for college; the multiple demands of her extended family; and her second husband's new career success, which required her to not only host more social engagements, but to be actively involved in her husband's business. She told me that she'd had breast cancer five years earlier and was doing fine around that issue with no reoccurrence. Kathy was a delightful, vivacious woman whom I enjoyed working with and therapy thus far had seemed to be helping her quite a bit.

On a Friday afternoon, about three months into our work together, I sat in a local coffee shop going over my caseload. Among other things, I was reviewing whether I was using sufficient mind/body tools with each of my clients, something I did regularly to help me from falling back into conventional therapy. When I came to Kathy's name, I found myself perplexed. She was a bright woman who was conversant with numerous alternative healing therapies. She had made clear to me how stressed she was, and I could see her distress in her body and voice during our sessions. Yet, thus far, I had not asked her to do any deep, relaxed breathing. Not once. I believed strongly in the power of breathing to uncover emotional truth and promote healing. Why hadn't I tried it with Kathy? I honestly didn't know.

At the start of our next session, I raised the issue with her. I told her that I'd been asking most of my clients to do some focused breathing, especially those who were demonstrating physiological stress. I wondered aloud why I hadn't asked her to breathe in any of our sessions. Then, I asked, "What do you think would happen if I asked you to sink into your body, relax, and do some quiet, deep breathing?" Kathy gazed off into the distance, her face grave and troubled. Turning back to me, she said quietly, "I would probably shake and sob."

Genuinely surprised, I asked why. "Because," she whispered, "I'm terrified that I'm going to die."

I asked her to help me understand what she had just said, staying with her breath as she did so. She told me that reaching the five-year mark of no cancer reoccurrence was not the relief for her that it was for many breast cancer survivors. Instead, for her it marked the point at which her youngest child left for college. She had vowed to live long enough to take good care of her daughter and provide her with a normal adolescence, of which, she had made good on that unspoken promise. Now that her daughter had left home for college, combined with the reality that Kathy was currently living a highly stressful life, she was sure that the time had come to pay her dues. She said, "I'm afraid that my cancer will come back—this time to take my life." Looking off into the distance again, she added quietly, "I think this is really why I am here."

We spent the rest of the session trying to unravel the thoughts and feelings—some rational, some not—that she'd pushed out of her consciousness until now. Kathy wept several times, sometimes with such raw fear and grief that my heart ached. She realized how hard she'd been pushing herself to get to that five-year mark, and how scared she was, now, that her most feared outcome would come to pass. The more obvious stresses that we'd been working with, such as her empty nest and extended family pressures, had mainly served to distract her from this elemental and deeply hidden source of stress—the terror of dying.

As the session continued, I realized that I, too, had been part of the denial system. Unconsciously, I had colluded with Kathy's desire to avoid her fear of dying. In hindsight, I recognized how I'd sat with her with an almost imperceptible level of stress in my own body, with my stomach and lower back tense and my hands slightly clutched. I realized that I'd kept my own breathing shallow, thereby not breathing fully into the tension I felt and avoiding awareness of it. Some unconscious part of me wanted to protect Kathy from facing, and feeling, the possible consequences of living with so much stress for so long. And the truth was, I was also trying to protect myself. I cared a lot about Kathy: I did not want her to have to feel the terror of facing the possibility of her death. After she got this clarity and processed her repressed fear she remained in therapy only a short time. The changes she needed to make in her life were clear and she didn't need my help to do it, just courage and the will to live.

It is an extraordinary thing that in our modern world stress is not merely accepted as a given but is often bragged about, as evidence that we've somehow "made it" in our fast-paced, achievement-centered society. Many of us have heard—or worse, taken part in—conversations in which one person somewhat proudly describes their high-pressure day, and the other responds, "Yeah, I know just what you mean," and then proceeds to one-up the other by reporting on their own, even more hectic and crazy schedule! We seem oddly disengaged from the well-researched, well-known reality that stress can cause serious, even life-threatening illness. Somehow, we haven't been listening.

If we chose to really hear a friend or partner talk of their chronic stress—heard it with our full, loving presence and consciousness—we would have no choice but to point out the likely consequences, eventual physical and/or mental health problems, and to ask them what they were going to do about it and ask how could we help them. Our offer of help might include showing them how to do some natural breathing, some positive healing imagery, and/or some simple qigong movements. We might suggest a class of yoga, tai chi, or mindfulness based stress reduction. How about this for a bumper sticker? <u>"Stress is a killer. Tell your friends."</u> And, if you're a friend to yourself, you'll extend the same loving honesty and care to your own body, mind and spirit.

CHAPTER 3:
THE MIND'S EYE:
USING IMAGERY TO HEAL

For the first two decades of my career, I had very little respect for the power of the mind to affect emotions. For the most part, I believed that people who used cognitive and other thought-based therapies were avoiding the "real work," the deep inner effort to discover, re-experience, and work through early sources of pain and dysfunction. It is quite humbling to admit this prejudice, because I have since learned that a focused mind that uses positive imagery is a formidable instrument. Through its capacity to change the human energetic system, imagery can have a tremendously positive impact on both emotional and physical health.

Looking back, I find it amazing that I managed to ignore the power of imagery for as long as I did. It certainly wasn't for lack of exposure. Back in graduate school, I had learned about the influence of the mind via pioneering research on depression by the psychiatrist Aaron Beck. He found that college kids who were suffering from depression were much more drawn to pictures of depressing topics than happy topics. Focusing on depressing images, in turn, tended to increase people's depression.[1] Beck and other proponents of cognitive therapy suggested that if you could help people focus on positive thoughts and images instead of negative ones, it could decrease depression and help to engender a sense of well being. I found this concept interesting, but certainly not compelling, and I really didn't believe it could lead to significant change for most people.

We also studied the placebo effect, in which people are given a pill without knowing whether it is a real medication or merely a "sugar pill" containing no beneficial ingredients. Studies consistently show that about 30 percent of individuals who take a sugar pill, or placebo, report the same rate of symptom improvement as do people who take the real medicine. In another indication of placebo power, a number of patients underwent doctor-recommended treatments for duodenal ulcers, herpes sores, and bronchial asthma, respectively. These particular treatments were later found to have no beneficial medical effect. Nonetheless, as many of 70 percent of these patients were healed by the treatment because they trusted their doctors' judgment and therefore believed that the treatment would be effective.[2]

Such is the power of the imagination. Yet in the graduate schools, where I learned about this exciting aspect of the mind, no professor ever suggested that we actually work with the thinking, imagining part of the human being, thus, I continued to dismiss imagery as irrelevant to the practice of therapy.

I was also aware of guided imagery and had experienced it in a few classes and workshops. But it seemed like "therapy lite" to me—a practice you employed to enhance your already positive feelings, guide you on your spiritual path, or perhaps help you through minor difficulties. Since I first became aware of imagery, research on the topic has exploded. Guided imagery has been found to significantly lessen anxiety and depression, reduce bingeing and purging in people with bulimia, and diminish the symptoms of post-traumatic stress syndrome. It also has been found to lower blood pressure, reduce cholesterol and lipid peroxides, speed healing from fractures and burns, decrease blood loss and length of hospital stay in surgery patients, and enhance numerous other aspects of health.[3]

I certainly didn't let this research disturb my prejudice. Nor was I influenced by the fact that I was using imagery myself! For several years, I had been practicing qigong and using peaceful, healing images as part of my practice. More and more, I was bringing these calming images in my daily life. As I waited in line at the supermarket on a Friday evening, or sat in my car battling rush-hour traffic, I would visualize myself relaxing in my backyard enjoying my gardens or sitting on my meditation pillow feeling totally at peace with life.

When I brought these images to mind, I could feel my tension begin to melt away and a sense of peace settle into my mind and body. Yet, as powerful as this practice was in my personal life, it never occurred to me to try to integrate imagery into my very traditional therapy practice. That is, until Colin walked into my office.

Seeing Red

Colin, a bright, articulate lawyer and a former client of mine, strode into my office looking like a bomb about to explode. I hadn't seen him in over a year. He sat down, looked at me grimly and said, "My marriage is finally over." I tried to hide my astonishment. I had done some intense couples therapy with Colin and his wife, Pat, for about two years, and when they'd left they'd seemed to be doing very well. I was very disappointed that things had gone downhill so far, so fast. "Tell me what's going on," I asked.

As Colin began to talk about his marriage, I noticed that his body was extremely tense. His shoulders were hunched up around his ears and his eyes were slightly squinted, as though the light hurt them. Every word he spoke about Pat carried a sharp, condemning edge. As he sat forward on the couch, speaking and gesturing forcefully, it was as though he were presenting his case not for discussion, but for certain conviction.

At first, he was pretty persuasive. Listening to him, I was distressed to hear of Pat's judgmental and passive-aggressive behavior toward Colin and her refusal to take responsibility for her behavior (which I knew to be her MO in conflict). I was regretfully coming to the conclusion that I'd missed something terribly important in my earlier therapy with this couple, some crucial, invisible reality that was now taking the marriage down.

As Colin continued to expound on Pat's lack of love for him, his face growing redder and redder as he spoke, I had an epiphany. I realized, suddenly, that Colin's mind—his image of Pat—was the fuel that was stoking his anger and stress response. My many years of practice, teaching and research on qigong came together in this moment with my therapy client. For 20 years of my professional life, I had denied the power of the mind in therapy. Yet here I was, witnessing the power of the mind in action, right in front of me.

I looked at Colin's blotched face, his flashing hands, his heaving chest, and I realized that his belief system was driving his emotional and physiological response, and vice versa. The more he imagined that his wife was "cold and unloving" and that his marriage was "killing" him, the more severely his stress response was triggered. In turn, the more stressed out he felt, the angrier he became. He was stuck in a continuous loop of body/mind fury.

In the past, with Colin (as with most clients), I would have intervened with psychological understanding. I would have probed for the early forces that had contributed to this current outpouring of anger and pessimism. For Colin, that would have meant revisiting his sense of abandonment by his critical and distancing mother, or his anger at his authoritarian father, or his unresolved grief about his failed first marriage. But sitting there with Colin, witnessing his rigid body and suffering face, I knew, suddenly, that my client needed an intervention that would speak to both his body and mind.

I started by asking Colin to stop his "ranting" for a moment. (I used that word on purpose to begin to challenge his thinking.) He stopped and looked at me quizzically. I asked him to just sit for a bit, breathe quietly, close his eyes and sink into his body and try and listen while I talked to him. He shrugged and nodded. Then, as he took a deep breath and closed his eyes, I summarized the case he had just made against Pat. I acknowledged her hurtful and frustrating behavior. Then, I presented what I knew about Pat's love for him and all of the positive efforts I'd seen her make in the course of therapy. I paused for a moment, letting him continue to breathe quietly. I then asked him whose view he thought was more accurate—the one he had presented, or mine.

Opening his eyes slowly, Colin said, softly, "I think yours is." He paused. "I mean, generally. But I know I'm angry for good reasons, too," he added, genuinely puzzled. I asked him if he would be willing to do what I've come to call "reality-based imagery"—a way of imagining your situation that is grounded in the ways things actually are in the big picture of your life, not the way you might wish or imagine them to be when looking at things through a single lens. (A single lens view of any aspect of our lives usually has a single story to it and usually limits us in negative ways.) When he agreed, I asked him to close his eyes again, and to breathe quietly and deeply.

I asked Colin to visualize the Pat I had just described, the one who'd been in this office with him and had truly wanted to work on her issues and build a good marriage with him. Next, I asked him to imagine himself and Pat entering their home together and looking back over the marriage during the last few months. "Just notice what emerges," I suggested.

Colin closed his eyes for a couple of minutes. Then his face twisted in a grimace and just as suddenly, it softened. When he opened his eyes again, he told me he now realized that the trouble had all started around a pretty big fight that had never gotten resolved. "We were standing in the kitchen arguing about how I had just reprimanded our oldest. I knew I had over reacted to him, but I was so defensive with her I just couldn't bring myself to admit it. And she was really letting me have it. I finally just walked away from her." He told me that he'd deeply felt Pat's condescension toward him, and he had felt too vulnerable to approach her afterwards. So he'd held back his feelings.

He saw how his resentment had grown and fed his old belief system—that his wife was mean, arrogant, and couldn't care less how her behavior affected him. He saw how this galloping resentment had created a distorted picture of Pat, one with just enough truth to get the fire of anger and blame going. He said that visualizing her sitting next to him on the sofa helped him see how unfairly one-dimensional and distorted his image of her had been. "That just isn't her anymore," Colin said softly. Through imagery he'd also seen how one-dimensional and distorted he had become, how his mind and body had fanned the flames of rage, and whipped up a conflagration that was now threatening to destroy his marriage. "Yuck, that isn't me anymore, either!" he exclaimed. Then he added, "At least I hope not."

But Colin was still perplexed. "Why would I get into such a tailspin when I know better?" he asked. I admitted that I really didn't know, but I suggested that he go back into the visualization, this time taking along his compassion for himself as his companion. I asked him to try to look at himself without judgment, with total acceptance of whatever came up in the imagery.

Colin closed his eyes and sat quietly for a few minutes. Then, with his eyes still closed, he whispered, "Wow." A couple of tears rolled down his face and then he opened his eyes. He told me he had been just watching how he'd reacted to Pat during and after the fight, trying to do it with compassion for himself.

He remembered, then, that this was his characteristic way of coping when he was depressed—to withdraw and blame Pat. He then realized that his depression had quietly crept back into his life—"like a little black cloud that's been growing above my head"—and that he needed to focus his energies now on attending to his depression, not on leaving his marriage. As Colin told me this, his body literally relaxed in front of me. Now he looked like a sad, depressed man. He was in pain, but he was, finally, in touch with himself.

In this session with Colin, I understood for the first time what I'd heard and read so many times—that the mind and body are deeply connected. Physical sensations can trigger thoughts; thoughts, in turn, can stimulate a powerful physical response. As guided imagery pioneer Belleruth Naparstek writes in *Invisible Heroes*, "Psyche and soma are simultaneously affected and utterly indistinguishable, one from the other."[4] The magic of imagery is that it can intervene powerfully on all levels. It can help us to quiet our bodies, let go of destructive emotions, and begin to see things from a different, more positive perspective.

Picturing Ourselves

Let's look for a moment at a type of imagery that all therapists and clients work with—the imagery of self. Each of us has a self-image, a mental picture of ourselves that we carry through life. Actually, we have several such pictures—some positive, some negative. Someone might have a picture of himself as a good dancer, a brilliant conversationalist, and someone who can arrange flowers quite beautifully. That same person may also imagine himself to be a klutzy skater, a stingy person, and someone stupid about politics. All of these images provoke an accompanying energy.

Of course, it's usually the negative self-images that clients bring into therapy. Every therapist is familiar with the problem of "poor self-image." What frustrates therapists and clients alike is that even after much good work has been accomplished—much self-understanding and working through of emotion—many clients leave therapy with a picture of themselves that is almost as negative as when they first walked in the door. They retain either a factual memory of how they were at some time in their past, or a synthesis of how they have felt over a period of time.

And this self-image is not a one-dimensional picture; it is a full-color, 3-D portrait. Years ago, I had a client who had done good therapy work around growing up as a victim of her mother's violence. Yet the minute she got into a fight with her partner, she would instantly experience herself as a pathetic little girl who deserved to be punished. I remember, too, a single man I worked with who had grown up in a large family with parents who were so depressed that they could barely attend to their own emotional needs, let alone those of their kids. This man had worked through his grief and longing to be cared for, had dealt with his anger, and had even forgiven his parents. Yet whenever he found himself alone on Saturday night, he plunged into depression and saw himself as utterly worthless.

Most therapists have seen this discouraging and puzzling phenomenon. Why is a poor self image so often impervious to change via the usual therapeutic methods—talking about it, understanding it, having compassion for it?

The answer, I believe, lies in the fact that we are fundamentally energetic beings. Through the study and practice of qigong, I have come to understand that a poor self-image impacts the energetic body and creates energy blockages in the body, which, in turn, suppress our natural sense of vitality and self-confidence. Because these blockages are part of our body's energetic memory, they are unlikely to be affected by talk alone. Imagery, by contrast, has repeatedly been shown to intervene at the physiological level (recall the studies on blood pressure, immune function, and pain reduction), as well as to affect thoughts and emotions. Let's take a closer look at how this works.

We All Need a Cheering Section

I'm currently working with Julia, a woman in her 30s who came to see me for relationship issues. Specifically, she feels she is never "good enough" for the men who want to date her. She feels very stiff and awkward around men and rarely gets past two or three dates with anyone. She has been obsessed with her weight for most of her life, and at one time was quite overweight. Now, she believes that she is at a healthy and attractive weight, but her self-image remains that of an "ugly, fat girl—somebody no guy would ever look at."

I have witnessed the toll this negative image takes on Julia. In a session, she'll be talking about something that trips that negative self-image, and immediately, she looks lifeless and despairing. Not only does she feel worthless, but also she reports feeling suddenly and profoundly exhausted, depleted of the essential energy she needs to feel empowered to change her life. She is aware that this happens when she feels "looked at" by me or when she is telling me about someone and pictures them looking at her.

Julia is now working on this issue in therapy by visualizing all the people in her life who are, or have been, loving toward her. She visualizes a bleacher full of these folks, each of them gazing at her with deep caring and acceptance, each of them knowing and loving both the former Julia who was overweight, and the current Julia who is the size she wants to be.

Just two weeks ago, I watched her change in front of me and fall back into that "ugly, fat girl" place of despair. All at once, her energy tanked—she looked like a tire that had just lost all its air. I asked her what had just happened. "It was when I saw you looking at me with kindness on your face," she said. "You looked like you really liked me, like you really thought I was a nice person." She looked very sad and alone as she stared at the floor.

I asked Julia if she'd be willing to try the visualization that we had been working with. When she nodded, I asked her to close her eyes, breathe, sink into her body, and begin to look at the bleachers filled with all of those warm, loving faces. I could see and feel her energy slowly return. Her face softened and regained color. Then she smiled and quickly blushed, still with her eyes closed. She laughed. I asked her what had happened. Opening her eyes, Julia said shyly, "I just put you in the bleachers." She had turned very red now, and wore the endearing look of a bashful 14-year-old. I couldn't help but blush back, caught up in feeling shy myself. She saw me blushing and we had a great laugh together.

Being loved, as we are.

A few years ago, I had a surprising and painful experience with my own self-image. Through a series of unusual circumstances, I decided to get myself tested for attention deficit disorder (ADD). I'd never thought of myself as having ADD, though I knew I was quirky in my thinking and processing of information. I certainly remembered difficulties back in high school—how hard it was to pay attention, how bored I was on some days, and how, on other days, I'd manage to understand what was taught, but somehow I couldn't get the information from my mind out onto the page. I flunked a lot of tests and almost did not graduate from high school. I remember teachers being very angry with me for "underachieving" and being a "lazy goof-off."

I'd come a long way since high school. After graduation, I found a very unconventional path on which to continue my education, and I eventually became a psychologist. I wrote articles, contributed to books, was an adjunct faculty member at a graduate school, and taught and spoke locally and nationally. So, who cared if I had ADD or not? I had made it.

It was, however, a little more complicated then that. When I was shown the test results confirming that I had ADD, I was surprised at the relief I felt. A lot of things were suddenly clearer—why I had put off college for several years, and why, when I finally did go, almost all of my classes were experiential rather than classroom-based. I now understood why I'd left the comforts of a group practice for the quiet of a private practice, as I found most people's need for order and process arduous and boring. (I mean, do we really need a meeting to discuss how much tape and paper clips to buy?) I understood better why I was attracted to intuitive therapy approaches rather than more linear models. On all sorts of levels, I began to make more sense to myself.

My test results also surprised me by bringing to the surface another part of me—the part that still felt like a loser, a stupid goof-off who was never going to make anything of himself. Lodged in the back of my mind and deep inside my energetic body was a picture of myself as a ninth-grade kid sitting in the back row of math class, slouched down in my chair at my desk, feeling worthless because I had just flunked another test. That image, and the heavy, despairing energy that accompanied it, had in some small way tainted everything I had accomplished, right up to the present. A little inner voice kept taunting me, "If people knew who you really were, they wouldn't be so impressed. Loser!"

Initially, I was astounded at the power of this image. I had already done a lot of healing work relating to my childhood and adolescence—the experience of growing up with two alcoholic parents and suffering low self-esteem and a shameful sense of self. But I recognized that this aspect of myself wasn't family-related. Instead, it was directly related to my ability to learn like others and "be normal" like others. I had never gone near this part of me before.

One night in my meditation, shortly after getting my test results, I quieted myself, sank into my breath, and went to a familiar image that I visited whenever I needed healing for something in my childhood. I visualized my beloved grandmother sitting next to me, and imagined she and I (the current adult me) looking at that kid slumped in the back of his math class. I visualized the two of us loving him for the quirky kid he was, knowing that his unconventionality was actually his gift to the world and that the adults around him just couldn't see it. I saw that kid with a little smile on his face, knowing the secret he was carrying and proud of the wonderful, bright, singular way that he walked in the world. I felt, too, my grandmother's love beaming into that boy at his desk, which made his smile grow even larger. As I sat there with acceptance, compassion and love for the kid with this neurological quirk (which felt much more loving than "learning disability"), tears streamed down my cheeks. I felt some part of my heart soften and open, his and mine.

Portable Healing

One of the great advantages of imagery work is that once you learn the basics, you can do it yourself, anywhere, anytime. My client, Clare, for example, customarily drives home in stressful, rush-hour traffic. During one recent drive home, she found herself snarled in freeway traffic and realized she would be quite late for dinner. She began to imagine how upset her husband, Michael, would be, since he was cooking dinner that night and had planned to serve promptly at 7 p.m. It was already 6:45 p.m.; she was nowhere near her exit.

Clare also knew she needed to talk with Michael that evening about plans for the upcoming holidays—specifically, should they invite her always crabby and depressed mother to stay with them for a few days? As her car continued to crawl down the freeway, she felt her body tightening and, oddly, found herself suddenly convinced that Michael would be hostile, combative, and totally opposed to her ideas for navigating the tumultuous waters of the holidays. She could actually see his thin-lipped face, his arms folded tensely across his chest. When Clare finally pulled into the driveway and walked through the front door, she felt angry, defensive, and ready for a fight. Guess what happened?

The next day, sitting in my office, Clare recognized that as she sat in the traffic jam, imagining being late for dinner and anticipating a difficult discussion, her stress response kicked in and, as a result, her thinking became increasingly negative. The more negatively she imagined her reception at home, the more stressed she became. Like Colin, she was caught in a mind-body stress loop.

I knew that teaching Clare to do some deep, relaxed natural breathing would be helpful; sensing that more was needed. Nearly every day, Clare had to drive home in bumper-to-bumper traffic that regularly increased her tension and with it, her angry, resentful imagery about her marriage and other issues. I sensed she needed some very powerful medicine—the medicine of positive imagery.

I asked Clare to close her eyes, breathe deeply, and imagine herself beginning her drive home from work. "What do you see and feel?" I asked. "As traffic starts to slow, I'm feeling my chest tighten," she says. "The muscles in my arms are tense. My hands on the steering wheel actually hurt."

I asked her what she might do to relieve that tension. "I'm putting on some soothing music," she said, her eyes still closed. "And now I'm starting to do some quiet, deep breathing, while I'm driving. I'm visualizing Michael having just cooked dinner for the two of us. He's waiting for me. His face is so disappointed! It makes me realize I needed to apologize for not leaving work earlier."

For a moment, Clare was quiet, breathing slowly and deeply. "Now I'm seeing all of the holidays we've navigated well together—all the Thanksgivings and Christmases with family," she said. "I see Michael understanding how worried I get about disappointing my mother." Clare paused again, continuing to visualize. "Michael looks concerned for me," she said. "He wants to talk about it." She stopped, and when she spoke again her voice trembled slightly. "We're sitting down on the couch together."

Since Clare was going home to a basically strong marriage, that beautiful visualization was pretty firmly grounded in reality. However, even if her marriage had been in constant conflict, she could still take actions that would significantly affect her mind and body. Just putting on calm music and breathing consciously during her drive home from work would begin to soften her defensive reactivity. Clare could then engage in some reality-based imagery about the upcoming evening with her husband. If she couldn't imagine Michael being receptive to her apology, or to talking about the holidays, she could visualize herself making amends for her lateness without defensiveness. She could then imagine herself staying grounded and honest in the discussion about the holidays. In short, Clare could do a lot to regulate her mind and body before she walked in the front door, regardless of what was waiting behind it.

Clare was able to quite quickly learn what we psychologists call "self regulation." This is the ability to maintain equilibrium of one's thoughts, emotions and behaviors. According to neurobiologist Daniel Siegel, "you can understand almost every mental health problem—anxiety, depression, eating disorders, personality disorders, thinking disorders—as an issue of self regulation."[5] Learning to use reality-based imagery is a profoundly simple and powerful tool for self-regulation. The more conscious we become of our reactivity, the more effectively we can use imagery to regulate our stress response and return to our natural state of calm energy.

Buddha observed that we create much of our own suffering. Life has inherent suffering, he said, but we make it much worse by the way we view ourselves and react to our life situations. One of the beliefs that causes us much unnecessary suffering is the conviction that we stand alone and separate from others. I have seen this image cause so much pain, both in my own life and in the lives of my clients, that I couldn't argue with Buddha's assessment. I think he was a strong proponent of reality-based imagery—the big-picture type.

In my experience, the practice of qigong helps us to let go of unnecessary suffering and embrace our lives more fully and joyfully. In every qigong exercise we do, be it the gentle movement of the body in an active meditation or a moment of sitting quietly, we always employ positive reality-based imagery—imagery that is realistic and possible, even if it is not yet present in one's life. Sometimes, it's as simple as imagining perfect energy flowing through our bodies. At other times, the imagery might be more specific, such as visualizing the anxiety or sadness in our heart area dissolve as we exhale. At still other times, it might be the image of feeling connected to our loved ones, or the people we happen to be with at that moment, or maybe even the entire planet.

My teacher often says, "If the imagery feels good in qigong practice, why not use it everywhere?" So, the next time you're sitting in a traffic jam, standing in line at the supermarket at dinner time on a Friday night, or walking into the office in the morning, try taking a couple of deep, slow breaths. Then, visualize yourself as calm and open to your experience. Try it out. You've got nothing to lose except your stress. And you have the world to gain—an inner world of growing joy, peace and equanimity.

THE SINKING BREATH

This next exercise is the one I most frequently use, both with my clients and myself. While similar exercises are often called diaphragmatic breathing or abdominal breathing, I simply call it the "Sinking Breath." This breathing practice relies much less on technique than on intention—the intention is to breathe naturally, which is a deep, slow, quiet breath. Qigong teacher and writer Stuart Olson eloquently expresses the simplicity of this Taoist breathing technique:

"The big secret is no secret at all. All that needs to be done is focus the mind on the lower tan tien (a spot deep inside the body behind the navel) and not on the breath; the breath will follow the mind. Mind does not follow the breath."[1]

So let's get started. Get comfortable, close your eyes and relax. Now, visualize a spot deep inside your body behind your navel, and imagine a small, bright white ball of energy there. Visualize your inhaled breath flowing into that ball of energy, making it brighter. Allow your exhale to happen naturally, without effort. Continue this practice for about 5 minutes, staying aware of what happens in your body. You may feel yourself relax, your breath deepen, or your mind quiet. You might become aware of physical sensations, or emotions, or nothing. You're not looking for anything in particular, just trying to be aware of "what is" as you ground yourself in your body.

Usually, I will teach this exercise once to a client, and then use a shorthand version after that. The next time, I will simply say, "Can you let yourself breathe as you sink into your body?" Eventually, I just say, "Can you sink your breath?" and the client knows what I am referring to. I will ask a client to do this exercise whenever they seem out of their body, too much in their head, or anytime that therapy seems off track. In my experience, this simple practice frequently helps clients to become more present to themselves.

The exercise can also offer a wonderful side benefit that the Taoists are so fond of offering us. With just the intention I mentioned above, inhaling to your lower tan tien, your abdomen and your lower back will tend to move slightly away from each other. If you don't experience this spontaneously, try visualizing the movement.

Why is this movement of the spine and abdomen more beneficial than merely extending the abdomen forward, as is usually taught in abdominal breathing? The reason is that the lower spine is a part of the body that tends to tighten up and lose its suppleness as we age. So by practicing this simple technique, you are keeping your lower spine more flexible, thereby extending the length of time in your life that you'll be able to tie your own shoes!

So wherever you are—on the bus, in the movie theater, walking around the lake—just take a few moments to visualize your inhaled breath traveling down to that spot deep in behind your navel. The Sinking Breath will help you keep your breath grounded in your body. And the more connected you are to your body, the more grounded and present you will be in your life.

CHAPTER 4:
ENERGY: AN INVISIBLE FORCE FOR HEALING

"Everything is energy," said Master Lin. He was standing at the front of the room, teaching our beginning-level qigong class. "Everything you do, say and think is energy. And all of it affects you." This was the first thing I ever heard Master Lin say about energy. It was a pretty big statement. Actually, a little too big for me at the time.[1,2] I really didn't get it, and I certainly didn't appreciate the power of energy in my own life. That soon changed.

A few weeks later, I became aware that most mornings while shaving, I would get into this negative thought loop about my exuberantly active son. I'd imagine Oliver leaving his bed a mess, forgetting to brush his teeth, and bounding out the door without his homework. As I shaved, I'd start thinking about these organizational lapses and feel my jaw tighten. Don't ask me why I got into this faultfinding mode while I was shaving—I never did figure that out. But after class one day, I asked Master

Lin why he thought I might be having such obsessively negative thoughts about my son, whom I loved deeply and didn't want to hurt.

He smiled and shook his head. "Patrick, it does not matter why you do it. You just change it." I suppressed a groan: How could he be so naïve and imagine it could be that easy? "When you catch yourself having those thoughts," he continued, "simply watch them turn into smoke, and replace them with kind, loving thoughts." Then, he added: "And, please do not go talk to a therapist about your negative thinking—they will make more of it than it deserves." His eyes were teasing, twinkling. But I knew that on some level, he meant it.[3]

Simplistic or not, Master Lin's prescription seemed better than none at all. So the next time I caught myself beginning to think about Oliver's inconvenient habits, I watched those images begin to fuzz around the edges, and then evaporate into smoke. I began, then, to consciously think about what I loved about my son—his openhearted delight in everything life offered, and the way his unstoppable curiosity invited me to share his sense of wonder about life.

I then encountered a new problem: it was very hard to shave while smiling. Before long, shaving had become a very different experience—a prelude to the enjoyable experience of sending Oliver off to school. As I helped him to get ready, I found myself relishing his energy and wild enthusiasm for the world.

It was a striking experience. I saw that my negative thoughts about my son had put me in a foul mood and left me chronically irritated with him as I sent him off to school. My positive thoughts, however, highlighted an entire different aspect of him, and left me filled with love and admiration. There was no doubt about it—changing my thoughts had shifted my energy.

Before long, I began to notice the connection between thoughts and energy in my work with clients. Most clients carry around negative thoughts about themselves and/or about others in their lives. Sometimes those thoughts are legitimate—they have lost a job, a husband is abusive, a wife is an angry alcoholic. People come into therapy to sort that stuff out. However, I began to recognize the distinction between acknowledging a difficult reality and creating energy around that reality. We can't always choose our reality, but we can always choose how we respond to it. That response, in turn, will have a powerful impact on our emotional and physical energy.

The Energetic Universe

As I mentioned earlier, the early Taoists were fascinated by the way that animals used and cultivated their energy, But in fact, they saw the whole universe and everything in it as a form of energy.[4] They believed that everything—people, plants, animals, every aspect of the natural environment, and even man-made objects—had their own, unique energy. A mountain has a certain energy, as does a lake. Moreover, each individual lake has its own distinctive energy. Sitting on the shore of one lake can evoke a sense of peace; sitting on the shore of another may leave us feeling neutral. By each lake having its own energy, each in turn, provokes a different energetic response in us. The same is true for different trees, birds, people, rocks, and so on. From this understanding of unique energies, the Taoists learned that the way structures are built—houses for example— and where things are placed in that structure creates a distinctive energy. (This is the basis of feng shui.) They also understood the energetic interaction between individuals and their environments. Why is it that some people like maple wood floors in their home while others feel more comfortable with oak? Why do some people prefer rose bushes in their front yards, while others plant lilacs? Why does one person like to dress in only light colors, while someone else always wears vibrant hues? The Taoists understood that we each have our own unique energy and that different elements help different people to stay in energetic balance. Our task is to learn for ourselves what daily choices, from living conditions and clothing, to friends, food, and so on—will help us live a more balanced life.

When Master Lin first moved to the United States, he just loved potlucks. We qigong students all would bring our favorite dish or dessert to someone's home, and he would stand at the table gazing at all the dishes like a kid in front of a Christmas tree. Along with enjoying the food and camaraderie, he would use these occasions to teach. At one potluck, as we all sat around with full plates in our laps, he talked about the energy of food. "When you practice qigong long enough and are willing to listen to your body," he said, "it will always tell you what it wants to eat." Personally, I was glad he'd said this after I'd filled my plate with all my favorite foods!

But when I'd finished my dinner and got up to look over the desserts, Master Lin's words were still fresh in my mind, especially his final suggestion: "You can practice this anytime, even today." I gazed hungrily at the half dozen or so offerings—caramel-covered brownies, chocolate chip cookies, chocolate cake, a chocolate-covered krispie-nut thing, and a couple of other visually tantalizing treats that weren't chocolate, so I don't recall what they were. As my mouth watered, I heard Master Lin's words: "Don't listen to your mind or pay attention to your senses, but ask your energetic body what it wants to eat."

Immediately, I knew that the brownie that my eyes, nose and tongue craved was not what my energetic body wanted. Unfortunately for me, it wanted more of the broccoli salad that sat right next to the brownies. Broccoli salad over a brownie? Give me a break! But as I stood looking at the food, I knew that my energy would feel so much better if I ate the nutritious salad instead of wolfing down one of those huge, delicious-looking, caramel-coated chocolate brownies. Reluctantly, I scooped a small pile of broccoli salad onto my plate. I hated to admit it, but afterward I felt good, not full or lethargic.

Over the years, I've learned to use this "energetic eating" paradigm, which is sometimes disappointing to the senses but heavenly to the body's energy. I don't drink much coffee anymore, because I know it will leave me jittery. While I love a glass of wine or a beer, I know it will leave me feeling woozy, so usually I forego that pleasure. I eat less food in general, and certainly less junk food and fast food. My body generally feels like a smooth running engine that has all the energy it needs, everyday for everything. I must admit that I do not always pay attention to my energetic body around chocolate or at potlucks. Unless, of course, Master Lin is there!

It's the Little Things That Count

Our energy is affected not only by our thoughts, but also by our personal environments. My client, Vince is a single, 33-year-old man in the fast-paced world of mortgage banking. He owns a beautiful home, a membership at a health club, a snazzy sports car, and a traumatic childhood upbringing that could easily keep him in therapy for years to come. He also has ADD, which is actually partly responsible for his career success. He is always thinking outside the box, and quickly. He is also one very stressed-out guy.

One afternoon in therapy, Vince was talking about the lack of any quality down-time in his life. He was on the go all day, visiting properties and conferring with clients and associates. His cell phone rang constantly. He told me that he craved his semi-annual trips to a friend's cabin in the mountains because of the sense of peace it brought him.

"The cabin sounds great," I agreed. "But are you satisfied with a semi-annual dose of peace?" Vince shook his head. So I asked him how much peace he found when he came home from work each day. He laughed wryly. "My house is as cluttered as my mind," he said. Vince went on to say that when he got home—usually late in the evening—he turned on only a couple of lights because he didn't want to see "how trashed" his place was. He described the scene briefly: newspapers and junk mail scattered everywhere, clothing littering the bedroom floor, empty beer bottles and crumpled packages of snack food here and there. "I actually like to cook," he told me, "but the kitchen is such a disaster zone that I eat out almost every night." He admitted that he often felt more exhausted at home than he did at work.

In the past, it never would have occurred to me to spend time talking with a client about his or her home environment. I would focus only on important "therapeutic issues." But it seemed obvious to me that Vince craved peace and was suffering from the lack of it, so I began to talk with him about the invisible toll that his home was taking on him.

I explained to Vince that his home environment possessed an energy of its own, a chaotic, agitated energy that was depleting him. However, the good news, I told him, was that it would be relatively easy to shift this energy. I offered Vince two simple suggestions. First, clean up your house, or have it cleaned, and keep it clean. Second, cook a nice meal at home at least twice a week. He looked doubtful; I could almost hear him thinking, "this is therapy?" "Just try it out," I said. "See what happens."

We have all experienced the calm, rejuvenated feeling that a clean house can give us. We know how much more pleasant it is to cook dinner when our kitchen is clean. We know the sense of order and well-being that comes from catching up on bill-paying and other household chores after we've enjoyed a good meal in our clean house, with perhaps some soothing music playing in the background. We usually don't think of the impact of our environment on our mental health—we just feel its impact. In qigong, we try to stay conscious of how everything we do affects our mental and physical health, including the way we maintain our personal spaces and carry out our personal routines.

Three weeks later, Vince walked into my office looking a bit more refreshed than I'd seen him in months. With a smile, he announced that he'd done his homework—literally. He had hired a cleaning service that had scoured his home from top to bottom two weeks ago, and with whom he'd arranged an every other week cleaning schedule. Once they'd left his house shining, he'd reclaimed his kitchen and had cooked there 3 times since then—everything from beef stew and chili, to his favorite dish, chicken cacciatore. We talked about how these changes could give him "a great return on his investment"—a language he certainly understood. Making small changes now, I explained, could contribute to the bigger changes he hoped for tomorrow. He nodded and said, "It's so nice to come home at night, make a good meal, and relax in my house!"

The Energy of Daily Life

Most of us don't realize it, but we're always responding to or manipulating the energy around us. An exercise I often do with clients and students is to ask them to look at the energy of their daily life. I walked them through their whole day, asking them to be cognizant of the energy of each and everything they do. I ask the following questions, which you may want to take a few moments to consider yourself:

How do you wake up in the morning? To a blasting alarm or quiet music?

What is your morning routine like? Do you give yourself enough time to do everything you need to do without being rushed? Do you eat a healthy breakfast, sitting down?

How is your drive to work—rushed or relaxed? What is the state of the interior of your car? What kind of music, news, or talk shows do you listen to on your way? What sort of energy do they leave you with?

Picture your office or workspace. Is it orderly? Are there any live plants? A good balance of different colors? How is the lighting—harsh, bright, dim, soothing?

How is your ride home? Ask yourself the same questions as you did for your drive to work.

After a day's work, what does it feel like to walk into your house or apartment? Is your home a warm respite, a sterile space, or a zone of chaos? Do you cook yourself a tasty, nutritious dinner?

How do you spend your time in the evening? Putsing? Watching TV? If you watch television, what sort of energy do the shows you watch leave you with? However you spend your time, do you generally find it restorative, or stressful, or empty?

When you allow yourself this kind of reflection, recognizing that you engage with the energy around you every minute of every day, it becomes easier to understand how energy can affect your mental health. In my own case, I have come to understand how the energy of my car affects my mood. While I try to keep my car environment as calm as possible, sometimes my mind is elsewhere and I just forget.

Take a couple of mornings ago. When I opened the car door, I immediately saw yesterday's cup of tea in the carrier, the cookie wrapper still crumpled on the front seat. There was also the magazine I took to lunch last week on the back seat, still sitting there because I hadn't been able to decide whether to bring it into my house or back to my office. My daughter's dance bag and empty water bottle from last night were on the floor. Then I turned on the radio, fiddling with the buttons till I came to a Van Morrison rendition of 'Gloria', a fast paced old rock tune. So within 10 seconds, I was submerged in the somewhat frenetic energy of the interior of my car. It only takes me five minutes to drive to work, but by the time I got there I was feeling a little hyped up, a little wired. I sometimes like that feeling, but walking into my office to spend the next hour sitting with a client is not one of those times. As I walked into my office building, I took some slow, deep breathes, shook my head, smiled, and told myself to practice what I preach, and to drive to work differently tomorrow.

Pause, Reflect, and Choose

We have more choices than we might imagine to shift the energy around us. Recently, one of my clients told me that she always went to bed right after watching the 10 o'clock news on TV. "I almost always feel depressed about the world afterward," she admitted. "But to not keep up on the news and hide from the world would be socially irresponsible. So I really don't have much choice." I asked her whether waiting to read relevant news stories in the newspaper the following morning would be irresponsible.

"I never thought of that," she said, laughing and a bit embarrassed. "I have always watched the news. But yeah, I could try that." Like many of us, she was attached to a daily habit and had never paused to consider other options. So often, all it takes to change our energy is a bit of reflection and a willingness to generate and try out healthier alternatives.

Slow Down, You Move Too Fast

In the qigong classes I teach, I talk a lot about rushing. So many of my students talk about how they rush to get from here to there, rush to get some project done, rush to get food on the table. Most of the time, they are convinced that they have to rush. I ask them, "How does your body feel when you rush? How often do you have clear, peaceful thoughts when you are rushing?" Usually, they laugh in recognition. Rushing makes it almost impossible to have a relaxed body and quiet mind.

The antidote? Become aware of your breathing. It is impossible to breathe consciously and rush at the same time. If you become aware of your breathing, you can still move along at a good clip, but you cannot rush. The reason is that if you're breathing well, your brain and physiology will simply refuse to rush. Conscious breathing gives your body a clear message: "This is as fast as I need to go."

I live 15 minutes away from that great cathedral to American consumerism, the Mall of America. The mall is a giant square of retail space, with mammoth department stores positioned in each the four corners, endless rows of small shops in between, and a loud, brightly-lit amusement park in the middle. I hate the energy of the place. I feel assaulted by the lights, the music coming out of most stores, and the hordes of people. Nonetheless, I find myself in this behemoth three or four times a year to take advantage of seasonal sales.

Like a lot of men, I take no pleasure in shopping. In the past, in an effort to get the whole annoying experience over with as soon as possible, I would rush from store to store, usually coming home exhausted and on the verge of a headache. I have since learned to walk through the mall while concentrating on my breathing. I still move along at a pretty quick pace, but I feel less frantic and more "in flow." I leave feeling less spent, energetically, than I have in the past. Sometimes, when I'm able to stay very grounded in my breathing, I leave feeling close to peaceful!

Every Choice Matters

As Master Lin said, "Everything you do, say, and think, is energy." When we pay attention to the small, daily details of our lives, we can choose to change our energy in ways that enhance our emotional and physical well-being. By making simple shifts in our habits—cleaning up the kitchen each evening, taking a less crowded route to work, choosing when to listen to Springsteen and when to tune into Vivaldi, appreciating something good in another person, and staying aware of our breathing, we can dramatically shift our experience of our daily lives. Working with our energy is that simple—and that powerful.

CHAPTER 5:
COMING HOME TO THE SELF:
A TAOIST FRAMEWORK

When I first started practicing qigong with my teacher, Master Lin, there was something about his philosophy that felt deeply inviting and comfortable to me. It was as though I'd plunged into a lake that I had longed to swim in for my whole life, without knowing it. I would learn that Master Lin's perspective came out of the Taoist tradition, and that along with viewing everything as energy, it offered a framework that continues to inform my life and therapy work. In both my personal and professional experience, Taoist principles offer a simple, powerful path toward emotional wholeness.[1]

Original Nature

Like most native peoples, the early Taoists of China carefully observed and learned from nature. One thing they noticed was that while particular animals might belong to the same "family group," such as robins, if you watched closely enough you would realize that each robin had its own individual way of being a robin. We would call this "character;" the Taoists call it their nature. They also used these observations to help them understand human beings. They came to the conclusion that we, too, possess an "original nature" that is unique to each individual. The task of our life, then, is to stay in balance with the energies within and outside us, so that we can live and respond to life from our original nature.[2]

When a client walks into my office, I start from the premise that they have somehow gotten off track and are no longer living from their original nature. What most clients are really asking me to do is help them come home to themselves. I believe this even when I hear the kind of plea that I heard recently from an anguished, weeping client named Wendy, "If I only knew what normal was, I would try and be it." I was pretty sure that becoming "normal" wasn't what Wendy was really hoping for. I suspected that what she really wanted was to be more truly herself, and to be comfortable and confident in her own skin.

Wendy told me she had spent most of her life trying to figure out the "right" thing to do in every significant intimate relationship. This strategy had failed miserably—all of her romantic partners had ultimately left her. I certainly recognized her grief in being repeatedly rejected, but I also assumed that part of her grief stemmed from her lifelong, frustrating and futile quest to figure out how to be "normal." I'm afraid to say, and glad to say, that we cannot achieve inner peace by trying to be anything other than whom we truly are.

Western psychology has many explanations for how we wander away from our inner self. Our personal experiences in our family systems, social worlds, and religious institutions are a few of the systems that influence our ability to follow our own nature. Of course, psychology is primarily focused on the individual's experience in his or her family. For Wendy, this experience included a poor attachment to her mother, a distant and abusive father, intense sibling rivalry, and a general lack of attention and acceptance in her early life.

Most schools of therapy I trained with would predict that I have a long-term client in Wendy, given the depth of her psychological and emotional wounds. However, the Chinese would look at this weeping woman quite differently. From one perspective, Taoists would see Wendy as a person who has strayed from her true nature. Rather than search for the sources of early emotional wounds, they would seek to identify the energy blockages in her body and to help her restore her natural energy flow. They might recommend healing approaches from all three branches of Traditional Chinese Medicine – acupuncture, qigong, and herbs. In my experience, combining qigong with my Western training is a powerful way to help clients return to their original, openhearted natures.

Getting Out of the Way

As Wendy sat weeping about her loneliness and her failed quest for normality, I knew that my first order of business was to get out of her way. She was so accustomed to looking to others for instruction on how to be, she'd lost faith in her own ability to look within herself for answers. Clients like understanding and insight; we all do, but that is not what Wendy needed most in therapy. Early in my career, I would have realized that the search for normalcy was foolish, but nonetheless I would have shared every insight I could muster about her search. I would have tried to educate her about the need to accept herself as she was. I would have explained that "normal" was actually pretty hard to find and not very pretty once you did find it. In short, I would have filled up much of the space around Wendy's longings and grief with my thoughts, my words, and me!

But now, listening to Wendy's plea and pain, I understood that something had gotten in the way of her natural energy flow, preventing her from contacting her core self. Thus, I needed to get out of Wendy's way so I could help her get out of her own way. Taoists often talk about self-cultivation as a process of subtraction, not addition. To get back to our original nature, we need to remove unnecessary obstacles rather than add on new knowledge or insight. Original nature doesn't flow from our efforts to figure out how we should be. Instead, it emerges when we impose nothing on ourselves except trying to keep our energy in balance and living from our heart.[3]

During the next few months in therapy, Wendy breathed and sank into her body every time she contacted that feeling of deep unworthiness. It was incredibly painful for her. She got in touch with the young girl who ached for her mother's attention, a mother who was so lost in her own misery that she had no energy left for Wendy or her other children. She also discovered a deep longing for her distant father, a father who would often react to her with brutal criticism and verbal hostility before retreating again into depression.

As we continued to work together, Wendy also began to recover her grief about her siblings, some of whom regularly put her down, and others whom she regularly put down. One afternoon in my office, Wendy realized that in addition to the part of her that didn't accept herself, there was another part of her that was very mean and judgmental toward others. Growing up, her older siblings had been quite cruel to her, and she had passed that right on to her younger siblings. "God, I was a shit to my younger brothers and sisters," she recalled. "I was so critical and nasty. I just hate that I took part in that."

Then, suddenly, Wendy made a crucial connection. She realized that part of what she'd resisted facing about herself was that she still had the capacity to be judgmental and unkind in relationships today. She saw that behaving "nicely" and seeking to "be normal" with men was not just an attempt to avoid rejection, but also a way of avoiding exposure as a "caustic bitch." She seemed painfully relieved when she told me this, and something in her seemed to relax, some tightness in her, some energy blockage, now seemed to be open and allowing her to be more present. Interestingly, some part of me also relaxed, some unconscious response I was having to her was now relieved that she was more present and less blocked up or held back.

As we further explored this issue, Wendy began to reflect on the way that this banished part of herself had distorted her career. She was a journalist who always wrote what she'd come to call "feature lite." She did nice stories about nice people that readers liked. "But I'm really drawn to more 'juicy' stories— stories that would stir the waters a bit," she admitted, smiling with pleasure at the thought. So, in my office, we worked with helping her to bring forward who she innately was—a bright, sharp, challenging woman—and helped her deal with how she had used that part of her to defend herself and hurt others, and to sort out from it the part that was innately her, her true nature, a part that needed to be "redeemed" as she called it. I will come back to Wendy later.

Feelings Are Not the Goal

Wendy was unusual in her willingness to face her pain head on. Too often, therapy clients fear getting in contact with their buried wounds because they're afraid they'll be "sucked in" by the feelings and never emerge. This was the case for Kevin, a new client who sat on the edge of his seat as he told me about his life. As he talked, I noticed that his eyes were bright with unshed tears.

Since graduating from college, Kevin told me, he'd had worked as an Emergency Medical Technician. He'd known he wanted to do this work ever since he was a little boy and had witnessed an ambulance pull up to a car accident and watched the men jump out of it and try to save the injured occupants of the car. Kevin, now in his 40s, was the oldest of several siblings who'd grown up in a physically abusive, alcoholic family. He told me he'd hated how powerless he was to help his younger siblings. Earlier in my career, I might have viewed this man's profession as a misguided way to try to save his wounded siblings. But Kevin's passion for helping people was so palpable that I had no doubt it was a part of his true nature.

So, then, why the tears? Kevin was deeply lonely. He knew no way to find acceptance except by trying to save others; he felt it was the only thing he had to offer of any value. In his zeal to help, he kept screwing up friendships, and he knew this aspect of him had also contributed to his recent divorce. The minute he found out that a friend was suffering, he began to treat them like a patient or a wounded brother or sister, offering a barrage of advice and embarking on rescue missions. As a result, many of his friends had retreated from him. He now spent most of his free time alone.

Yet, I suspected that there was another piece to the puzzle. When I asked Kevin if he had ever been attended to with the care and tenderness he extended to others, tears flowed down his cheeks as he shook his head. But quickly, Kevin stopped crying and looked very embarrassed. He told me that his grief and longing to be cared for left him "feeling like a six-year-old" and that he couldn't bear to feel so vulnerable. A couple of sessions later, he began to talk about his father's violent bouts of beating him and his brothers. At one point, choking back long-held sobs of terror, Kevin gasped, "It's just too much. I can't take it. I don't want to get in touch with all those feelings. They'll never end!" Now he was openly weeping.

As an Irishman and a psychologist, I had always put great stock in cathartic release. I believed that getting in touch with your feelings would help you contact your true self. The bigger the emotional release, the closer to home you got. Conversely, Master Lin taught me that the Taoists are not so impressed with these moments of great emotion. They see potential danger in the single-minded pursuit of "getting in touch with feelings" because it can lead a person to use their feelings as a major orienting principle. This, in turn, can lead to an over-focus on oneself, and too little focus on others and the world. But Taoists don't turn away from emotion, either. They believe in neither denying nor attaching to feelings. Feelings are just part of the natural wave of our humanity, rising and falling in a continuous, flowing rhythm.

So in therapy, I try my best to be present and help clients accept whatever comes. Because it's therapy we're doing, what often comes are feelings—sometimes big ones, sometimes unexpected ones. I remind my clients that experiencing feelings is not the goal, but just part of the ebb and flow of life and healing. The Taoists believe that the dark clouds and storms of nature are as important as the blue skies and sunny days. My main task is to get out of the way, help them get out of the way, and allow the waves of emotion—both stormy and gentle— come and then go.

I told Kevin that getting in touch with a lot of repressed emotions was probably part of what would happen in therapy. But, I said, what he most needed was a coming home to himself, a safe, grounded place from which he could confidently live his life. What he was after, I explained, was much larger than the part of him that had been abused and neglected. It also included his goodness—as an EMT professional, father, brother, son, and man. "Finding that place," I told him, "will help you to know much better how to walk in the world, be with others, love and be loved."

When Kevin heard that, his whole body relaxed, and tears once again sprang to his eyes. "I'm so tired of trying so hard to fix everybody," he said softly. As we continued to work together, Kevin allowed himself to process what emotions came up for him, and that included a lot of old, intense feelings of grief, terror, anger and loneliness. What also came was a feeling of being able to be strong and grounded in the midst of a storm, which he described as being like "a big oak tree that sways with the wind and storms, but stays steady." He liked that feeling a lot. From this place Kevin began to experience the depth of his longing for care and love, and slowly, he began to allow others to nurture him. As he put it, "An oak tree has to have sun and rain to survive and to thrive."

Right Effort

The Taoists believe that once we are grounded in our true nature and in balance with our energies, we will naturally bring the "right effort" to everything we do.[4] In Chinese, this concept is known as "Wu Wei," which means no action, right action, or right effort. Sometimes, "right effort" involves doing a lot, while at other times it means doing nothing at all. My client, Kevin, often did more than he should, often alienating others because he intruded too far into their worlds. Wendy, for her part, was putting tremendous energy into trying to be someone that others would approve of. Her strenuous program to change herself and be "normal" certainly involved effort, but not "right effort."[5]

Those of us who are therapists know a lot about right effort, though we may not call it that. When we try too hard with a client, it is rarely helpful. When we are removed, it is likewise not helpful. I always find it refreshing, though sometimes embarrassing, when a client chides me for seeming to be "not there"—not paying attention, looking tired and distracted, or otherwise not being actively present with them. More often than not, their assessment of me is inaccurate and reflects more on the particular issues they're struggling with. But sometimes, my clients are right—my mind is elsewhere. They are saying, "Hey, I'm paying good money to be here, I need your help and you're not bringing enough effort to the task. So shape up!" That is usually the right effort on their part—telling the truth about their here-and-now experience and trying to re-engage me.

One evening, while taking a call at home, I hollered at a client. Literally hollered at him. I watched myself as I did it, conscious that not a single teacher or supervisor I'd ever had would support what I was doing at that moment. But it didn't stop me a bit—because it felt instinctively right. I had been seeing Brian for about three years and we'd done some very good work together, especially on some tough family-of-origin issues. However, at this moment, on the phone, he was telling me that he and his fiancée were tired of his "crazy fucking family" making it impossible to plan their wedding, so they were just going to skip the whole thing and elope over the coming weekend. He added, by the way, that he had no time to come in and see me for the rest of that week.

Brian's story was complicated, involving lots of early deprivation and lots of continuing control issues with his parents. I didn't argue with his assessment of his parents. I could really understand why Brian would want to elope, but I also absolutely believed that he would regret it for the rest of his life. So when he blew off my initial, calmly-stated objections, I started raising my voice and then really lit into him. I told him that eloping was wrong, selfish, and harmful to everyone— including him. I told him this act of passive aggressiveness would undermine the support and blessings from all of his friends and relatives who weren't "crazy controlling bastards"— but people who loved him, people whom he wanted and needed to stay in his life.

As I wound down, I told Brian that I cared too much about him not to let him know the depth of my feelings. I told him he was stronger than he imagined and had more integrity than to pull off something like this. To his credit, Brian heard me out and was clearly taken back by the strength of my feelings, but what I didn't know was whether he would change his mind.

Brian came in the following week, still single. Without a word, he sat down and began to weep. Afterward, drying his eyes on his shirtsleeve, he told me that when I'd yelled at him on the phone about eloping, "it was the first time I'd ever felt any real fathering." He said that it had felt wonderful to feel the strength of my beliefs wrapped around my care for him. He was glad, too, that he'd made the decision to work through the family issues surrounding the wedding, as trying as that would be.

For my part, I am glad that I trusted my gut, got my psychologist mind out of the way, and did what seemed so effortlessly right. And I really hope I never have to holler at a client again.

Home is Where the Heart Is

A key tenet of Taoism is that all physical and emotional problems are caused by energy blockages. When I first heard this unfamiliar concept from Master Lin, I was full of questions. "So, if someone is anxious, where is that blockage in their body?" I asked. He said, "the heart." Then I asked, "What about depression?" Again, he responded, "the heart." "How about anger?" He replied, "the heart." "Excessive sorrow?" Same thing. "And trauma?" Most definitely, "the heart." Master Lin's responses perplexed me for some time. To be honest, they seemed more than a little simplistic. How could every significant emotional problem be traced to a blockage in the heart?

After several years of learning and practicing qigong, the obvious became obvious. Every emotional struggle we have in some way impedes how "openheartedly" we approach life and respond to the people around us. Certainly, anxiety makes us too uptight to be very open. The same goes for anger. When we're depressed, there is not much energy available to flow from the heart. Excessive sorrow leaves us too engulfed by our own struggles to open ourselves to others. As for trauma, we are usually too focused on protecting ourselves from further trauma to risk being very open. Once I thought about emotional struggles this way, I realized that most of my clients were really coming to therapy to ask me to help them open their hearts. Interestingly, viewing my clients this way has helped me have a more open heart to everyone who walks into my office.

Once I understood that all emotional and psychological problems caused an energy blockage in the heart, I expected that addressing these problems from an energetic, or qigong, perspective would resolve them relatively quickly and easily. Master Lin had said this would be the case if a person began to address the blockage as soon as it occurred. Unfortunately, by the time most people come into therapy, their heart energy has been blocked for quite some time. Consequently it frequently takes time—sometimes a lot of time—to clear the blockage and restore the free flow of energy. But in my experience, the results are well worth the effort.

So, let's come back to Wendy. As I mentioned earlier, she had learned to sink into her breath and body whenever she fell into a sense of unworthiness. In that place, she found a lot of pain and longing for care. Once she let herself see that she could also be mean and judgmental, she began to breathe and sink into those feelings as well. Slowly, after a lot of struggle, she came to a place of not just insight, but acceptance of herself.

In the past, I would have thought that this was a good-enough place to come to; I no longer believe that. Self-acceptance isn't necessarily compassion, and only compassion for oneself has the power to transform who we are and how we walk on the earth—and compassion can be found only in the heart.

I remember the day that Wendy contacted this place inside of her, because as she left my office, I looked out the window onto a kind of Norman Rockwell scene. Snow was falling softly and peacefully, painting the trees and bushes with delicate designs. As I gazed out at the newly gilded landscape, Wendy's last words of the session danced in my ears and in my heart. With a radiant smile, she had said, "I really didn't believe I could ever feel this way about myself. Ever."

Wendy had been reflecting on her therapy process up to this point, talking about the difficulty of facing the abuse and deprivation she came from, and how especially difficult it was to come to terms with the "caustic bitch" she'd been hiding from. She realized she had spent most of her life hiding from that part of her by clinging to the image of herself as a victim of her parents—a pure, total victim. But now she was no longer using the victim stance as a defense against recognizing the harm she'd caused others. Among other steps, Wendy had found a spiritual director in her Episcopal church and had begun to learn to pray and to have a more intimate relationship with Christ. She was feeling good about what she'd been able to do, as she should have. Then I invited her to go further.

"Wendy," I said, "you have done incredibly well in therapy, and it shows. You have used your mind and body to support you in your healing. You are in a good place and I'm happy for you. But knowing you and how you have integrated all this healing, I think that you can take this a step further. I think we can do a better job of bringing your spirituality into your healing, a process I call sinking into your heart."

Her face brightened and she seemed eager to continue. I invited her to begin the familiar process of sinking into herself, breathing slowly and deeply. But this time, I gently said: "Focus on sinking into your heart, the place of love and compassion. View your whole life—from your childhood right on up to the person you are now—from your heart." She closed her eyes, took a big breath, and then was quiet for three or four minutes.

When she opened her eyes, she said softly, "I think I need to put Jesus next to me. I don't feel strong enough to do this on my own." I remembered her telling me, earlier, how powerful and helpful her praying had been. "Great," I responded. "Trust yourself and do it in a way that works for you."

She closed her eyes and in within a couple of minutes, her face broke into a small, sad smile. Tears began to stream down her face. I sat quietly, just trying to be present with her, with my heart open.

Wendy sat silently for 10 or 15 minutes, her eyes closed. Sometimes, her face reflected a deepening sadness; other times, she wore a loving smile. Off and on, tears ran down her cheeks. When she finally opened her eyes, they were softly glowing. "I just felt such love for myself, for all of us kids, growing up," she said, almost whispering. "But I felt it even for my parents. God, everyone was in such pain. And I can even see myself now, trying so hard to find 'normal,' but really just trying find love. And at this moment, with Christ sitting next to me, it feels so easy to love myself."

"I really didn't believe I could ever feel this way about myself. Ever."

Healing is Part of our Nature

In important ways, our emotional body is no different from our physical body. When we have a cut on our arm or a nasty sinus cold, our physical self knows exactly what to do to heal the wound or to attack the virus within us. All we need to do is give the body the best conditions possible—plenty of rest and good nutrition—to do the job it naturally knows how to do. Emotionally, things operate pretty similarly—the emotional self knows what to do to heal itself, so long as we grant it the space and permission to do so.

We see how children, given a safe-enough environment, allow themselves to respond naturally to the emotional vagaries of life. When they're sad, they cry. When they're happy, they laugh. Those of us who are parents can remember when our young child would be playing quite contentedly, and then, suddenly, toddle over and jump into our arms to be held. The child would burrow in for a few moments, and then, replenished, would push off to resume playing.

This ability to respond freely to our emotional needs is within all of us. But as adults, few of us can readily express our emotional truth. As we moved out of early childhood, we learned that it was no longer okay to cry when we felt sad, no longer okay to be exuberantly joyful in certain situations, and certainly not okay to jump in someone's arms when we needed love or comfort. Not all of this behavioral education was necessarily harmful; we may not always need to weep outwardly to express sorrow, nor get comfort only in another's arms. But too often, we experience a significant split between our outward, socially-approved life and our inner, emotional one.

When I was 15, my favorite grandmother died. I was heartbroken. Among her grandchildren, I was one of two "black sheep" on whom she'd bestowed special love, care and acceptance. For me, the experience of being so unconditionally loved was intoxicating, and I felt a tremendous loss at her passing. But I was told that I would be one of her pallbearers, and it was made clear to me that at her funeral, I was not to cry. "Be strong and don't embarrass us," was the unmistakable message. My sorrow felt huge and raw; I was horrified at the thought of carrying this wonderful woman to her grave. But I did what I already had plenty of experience doing—I repressed my feelings. I did not cry at my grandmother's funeral. Instead, my grief lodged in my heart, leaving an energy blockage there.

Many years later, in therapy, I began to talk about my grandmother. To my horror and shame, a wave of grief erupted from me as I remembered her sheltering love, and the loss of it. Desperately, I tried to control my feelings. I looked down at the floor and sort of froze up, wanting to cry but feeling deep shame at the thought of me, a grown man and a new psychologist, weeping. Meanwhile, my therapist was very quiet, which worried me. Was he judging me, thinking I was weak and out of control? Finally, I looked up, and to my astonishment, I saw tears in his eyes. At that moment, I knew it was finally safe to do what my body had naturally wanted to do on that day two decades earlier, when I carried my beloved grandmother to her grave.

Looking back on that moment, I see that my therapist had gotten out of my way. He didn't try to analyze me, educate me, or exhort me to "feel my feelings." Instead, he made a very subtle, human "right effort" in letting me see the tears in his eyes. That simple act of humanity helped me to get out of my own way, by freeing me from my shame. As I wept that afternoon with my therapist sitting by my side, I remembered how it felt when my grandmother walked into the room and cast her warm, loving gaze on me. It was as though she was seeing directly into the goodness inside of me, and it had melted the walls around my heart. After my therapy session, I felt a greater acceptance and appreciation for the tender-hearted boy inside me and for the loss he bore. As I walked to my car, I remember feeling as though my heart were bigger somehow. I felt more expansive, more alive.

This is the gift of coming back to the natural self. When you get out of your own way and allow your natural self—your original nature—to come forth, there is no room for self-judgment or self-improvement projects. Even if you anger more quickly than the next person, or if you're more excitable, or if you're more introverted, so what? What is right effort for you may be very different for someone else. You wouldn't be judgmental of the difference between Alaska and Hawaii (even though you might prefer one over the other), nor would you make a moral judgment about the plants that grow in a Northern climate versus those that flourish in a Southern climate.

For the Taoist, a human being has as much claim to his or her natural self as does a mountain, a lotus flower, or a flowing river. When you are grounded in your original nature, there is no more striving, no more struggle. You are in your heart. You are home.

E   X   E   R   C   I   S   E   T   H   R   E   E

THE GROUNDING BREATH

Now, let's do a standing breathing and imagery exercise. The first part is particularly helpful for people who want to feel more grounded or embodied in their lives. The second part, which incorporates arm movements, can be especially helpful for those with very active minds or who are coping with stress and/or anxiety.

Part 1: Inviting Energy

Start by standing with your heels parallel, about shoulder width apart. Bend your knees slightly and tip back your pelvis a bit (which straightens the spine). Relax your shoulders and tuck in your chin just a tad.

Then, imagine that you have a string attached to each of your elbows, and that someone is pulling those strings outward about 3 or 4 inches, just far enough so your hands are no longer touching your legs. Spread your fingers so that they are slightly apart. Each of these little body placements will help your energy to flow better. But if you find any of these instructions confusing, just do what you comfortably can. As long as you stand and find a position that you find relaxing, the exercise will work.

Now, as you inhale, visualize energy moving into your body and settling deep in behind your navel. You can visualize the energy of the inhaled breath as rising up from the earth, or as flowing from all directions into every pore of your body. Do what works best for you. With the exhale, you can just relax and visualize the exhaled breath helping to release your stress, worry, or other unneeded energy.

For clients who feel depressed or otherwise disconnected from their bodies, I suggest that they take time in this posture to sense each part of their body, from their feet up to the top of their heads. You may want to guide clients in this part of the exercise, i.e., "Now, notice any sensations in your feet...now in your lower legs," etc. Once they feel in touch with their body, I suggest that they then visualize (because often they can't yet feel) the dynamic energy in their body. This practice helps them to begin to experience a sense of being present and alive.

Part II: Ball of Energy

From your standing position, keep your upper arms and elbows at your side and lift your hands so they come up in front of your body about waist high, with your palms facing each other, about 6 to 8 inches apart. Imagine that you are holding a ball of energy in front of you. Notice if it has color, and the way it feels in your hands.

As you inhale, imagine that ball expanding as you allow your elbows to guide your hands out to the sides of your body. Then, as you exhale, bring your hands back to their starting position, a few inches apart. As you bring your hands back toward each other, visualize yourself compressing the ball. Your imaginary ball moves something like an accordion, expanding with your inhale and contracting with your exhale. As you continue the practice, see if you can feel the energy pulsing between your hands.

Again, visualize an image of energy coming in that feels good to you, and as you exhale do the same. A popular one we use in qigong, and I recommend to my anxious clients, is as you inhale visualizing good pure energy coming into your body through all your pores and then gathering in your lower tan tien (behind the navel) and then as you exhale visualizing all stress and anxiety turning to smoke and leaving out your heart area, in the middle of the chest.

This movement tied to the breath and imagery are often helpful to clients because it helps them to focus their mind, move out of obsessive thought patterns and begin to release their stress and anxiety. It also slowly helps people learn to breath more deeply, slowly and quietly.

Section 2:
Healing the Self

CHAPTER 6:
BEYOND WORDS:
PSYCHOTHERAPY FROM THE
MIND, BODY AND HEART

Most of the time, I love doing psychotherapy. But occasionally, it can be very frustrating. When things move painfully slowly—or not at all—it can be a real challenge to stay present. There's a temptation to blame the client; Why can't she focus? Will he never face his problems? But after 30 years of doing therapy, I know that my frustration can usually be traced to one of three ways that I'm relating to my client.

The first way is when I try too hard. A client's resistance to change is a normal part of most therapies (something I will address further in the next chapter), and my frustration stems from the fact that I'm putting too much effort into trying to bust through that resistance. I'm offering insights they are not ready for, or encouraging them to sink into emotions that may overwhelm them, or maybe challenging them in hopes of igniting some passion that may or may not be below the surface. Instead, I need to find and apply "right effort," which might mean sinking into my breath, having more compassion for why my client is struggling, or reflecting on what is getting triggered within me.

The second reason my frustration in therapy is my own grandiosity. Directly or indirectly, my client has asked me to help him or her with the impossible, and for some reason I have directly or indirectly agreed. This usually happens when a client asks my assistance in making an enormous emotional, spiritual, or life change without understanding that reaching this goal will involve more than sitting on my couch for one hour per week. Now they are unhappy that more is not happening more quickly.

In such situations, my task is to get humbly off my white horse and get honest with my client about the amount of effort and persistence these hoped-for changes will entail. Usually, this straightforward explanation is very sobering for a client, while at the same time freeing me from feeling responsible for their life. Thankfully, with age and experience, these flights of grandiosity on my part have gotten fewer and farther between.

The third, and most common source of frustration for me—and probably for my clients as well—is when I allow therapy to involve too much talk. It's hard to avoid the trap of over-talking in therapy; after all, many of us call what we do "talk therapy." Generally speaking, we Westerners like to understand and verbally process our emotional dilemmas, at times *ad nauseum*. (Master Lin often shakes his head and says, "Patrick why do you people think you need to understand everything? Sometimes, you just change it.")

But we are who we are. Most people come into therapy to talk, and the truth is, I like talk therapy. It has been helpful to many people, including me. But as much as words can help to explain, they can also drain meaning. In their beautiful book, *Grace Unfolding: Psychotherapy in the Spirit of the Taoteching*, Greg Johanson and Ron Kurtz write:

> From the outset, the Taoteching [the Taoist bible] points to both the inevitability and the inadequacy of words. In psychotherapy, the words we use both give rise to and kill meaning. Words can name and create meaning, bringing experience to expression and understanding. However, they never capture precisely what is. We can get lost in words. They can separate us from experience, imposing alien meanings on it instead of being congruent with it.[1]

I sometimes call myself an Irish storyteller therapist, one who helps clients discover and tell and live the passionate, accurate stories of their lives. Words have always had—and still have—the utmost meaning to me. Again and again, I have seen and heard the right words connect people immediately with their experience of themselves, their story, and the healing that needs to happen. What clients need to find is resonance, and this happens when the words they speak carry such conviction that you know they come not just from their mind and mouth, but from their whole being.

For many years, language was the only tool I had to discover resonance. I didn't know, then, that the resonance I was looking for could also be called a mind/body connection. I had only the mind, or words, to work with, and didn't understand that I also needed to help my clients hook up to the truth their bodies carried; a truth that would begin to open up their energy blockages and allow their vitality to freely flow.

Instead, my clients and I would wrestle endlessly with words, hoping they would eventually open the door to an experience of their authentic selves, an experience encompassing both mind and body. While some clients were able to arrive at this place quite easily, many others struggled mightily, and I was limited in my ability to ease their way.

The Language of the Body

So, like many things in life, talk therapy can be both a blessing and a curse. When I get frustrated with therapy and am pretty sure it's because we're over-talking something, I ask myself, "Is there some way I can use the mind/body paradigm to help my client become more present to himself or herself, and to help the therapy get moving again?"

Just a few weeks ago I was in session with a middle-aged man named Thomas, who was telling me of the terrible experience of his sixth-grade teacher mocking him because he had stuttered in class. He told me that "my teacher really shamed me," but as he said these words his tone was flat, without any resonance. I encouraged Thomas to look for a word that had more meaning for him and would connect him more deeply with his experience. I probed—had he felt his teacher's contempt, loathing, ridicule? Had he felt assaulted, attacked, cornered? Both of us started working very hard to locate the "right" word that would accurately describe his experience and, in the process, open a door to more expeditious healing. But we weren't finding that word, and both of us were getting pretty frustrated.

As you've no doubt noticed, I was going at Thomas's issue with my old paradigm, looking for resonance only through the hard work of cognition and talk. I have seen some clients become a bit overwhelmed by my probing; I've witnessed others struggle to find the right word just to please me. Certainly this is not "right effort," either for them or for me. When I realized what I was doing with Thomas, I knew that I needed to help him connect with his own experience; I knew I could only do this by getting out of his way.

So I asked Thomas to sink bodily into the experience of his teacher's mockery. "Listen to your body and breathe," I suggested gently. "Trust that your body knows exactly what your teacher did to you." I sat back as Thomas took slow, quiet breaths for a couple of minutes. Then, with a pained face, he muttered, "The fucker was absolutely disgusted with who I was."

That word, "disgusted," which he said in a tone dripping with contempt, seemed to resonate in him from the top of his head to the tip of his toes. It quickly led to anger, then grief, about the cruelty of his teacher and its impact on his life. What was powerful for both Thomas and I was that he came to this clarity entirely through following his bodily experience, rather than trying to "figure it out" via his mind.

Clients like Thomas help me to appreciate the potent, image-laden language of the body. In *The Tao of Breathing*, Dennis Lewis tells us "the body we know so well is in large part a 'historical' body—a body shaped by the past, by the results of long-forgotten physical and emotional responses to the conditions of our early lives."[2] So when I sit with a client like Thomas, not only am I sitting with someone who has been shaped by 20 or 30 years of habits in his adult life, but also by 20-odd years of conditioning before that, much of which lies beneath consciousness. No wonder I have been frustrated with the limits of talk therapy! Talk is important, but it is rarely enough.

Over the years, I have used certain disciplines to help me expand my traditional therapeutic approach to incorporate what I've learned in qigong. One of these disciplines, which I mentioned earlier, is to stop by my local coffee shop at the end of each week to spend some quiet time going over my entire caseload. With each client, I ask myself whether employing some breathing, imagery, or other qigong techniques might help the therapy process. For several years, I also was part of a peer consultation group that discussed clients from a mind/body perspective. This helped me move away from viewing clients primarily through the lens of their diagnosis – their neuroses or pathologies – and begin to experience them in a fuller, richer way.

By far the most effective method for changing my therapy approach has been the most direct method—changing myself. Before each session, I quiet myself and call up an image of my next client. For example, I might see my client Sid as an uptight and angry man, or Zoë as a depressed woman with a blank, hopeless look on her face. I then sink into my breath and body and into my heart and look at my client once again. Now I'm able to see Sid as a very insecure, fearful man who is hoping that I can see past his anger and into his goodness and help him find a different way to be with people. When I refocus on Zoë, I see her pleading with me to help her live a more active and passionate life, one in which she warmly and easily connects with people rather than shrinking from them. These altered perceptions probably would have come to me anyway in the course of a session, as I witnessed my clients' pain and struggle. But now they are with me as I greet each client at the door, my heart welcoming their heart.

The Mind/Body of the Therapist

I've said it before, but it bears saying again: Every therapist can benefit from some sort of regular mind/body practice. Certainly, it's possible to get your client involved in breath work or reality-based imagery without having a mind/body practice yourself, but its efficacy will be limited. If you ask your client to take deep, slow, life-filled breaths while you're taking shallow, quick, lifeless breaths, imagine the message that this conveys to the client, however unconscious. Or, if you ask your client to visualize a life filled with love and hope, while at the same time you're holding an image of your client's limited capacity for change, imagine how that gets in the way of their healing. When we're able to practice presence and openheartedness, we will be better prepared to help our clients do the same.

A mind/body practice can also be a powerful diagnostic tool for the therapist. As I sit with clients, I always try to ground myself in my breath and my body. After many years of doing this, it now comes pretty easily. So when I find myself experiencing certain sensations in a session, I ask myself, "What are these sensations telling me about the client?" If I notice some tension or anxiety in my body, perhaps the client is getting close to some emotional material they are scared about. On the other hand, if I notice that I'm breathing shallowly, maybe I am bored. If so, I reflect on where and why the client may have "unplugged" from themselves, and in so doing, pulled the plug on their connection with me.

Imagery works in the same way. If, in a session, I flash on an image of my client in some deep emotional state—perhaps weeping or cowering—I know I'm picking up some unspoken energy in the room. If I can be reasonably sure that the imagery isn't grounded in my own psychic material, I look at how it may illuminate what is really going on with the client, underneath the surface of talk. Sometimes, that reality can be quite startling.

A few years ago, I was working with Dave and Jeannie, a young couple who were engaged to be married and had come to see me because of conflicts around communication. Both had come from very wealthy families and were highly educated, gracious, well mannered—and almost impossible to help. I was working hard, pushing them to be a lot more honest with each other. In response, they would stubbornly deny any negative feelings toward the other person. I still remember Jeannie saying stiffly, "I am not frustrated with Dave wanting more time alone. I am fine with him needing his space. I need mine, too. I just wish he would let me know ahead of time so I wouldn't make plans for us to get together with other people." As she spoke, she stared straight ahead and twisted her hands in her lap.

One day, while sitting with this uncommonly courteous couple, I realized I was breathing very shallowly, leaning slightly forward in my chair with my legs and arms slightly tense. The third time I became aware of this in a 10-minute period, I decided it was worth paying attention to. So I took a deep, slow breath and asked myself, "What are you anxious about? What might be going on right now that is making you so tense?"

Suddenly a visualization popped into my head. I saw these two seemingly pleasant people turn on me and begin to violently rage at me. I saw them shaking their fists in my face, shrieking and cursing. Instantly, I knew what was going on. Neither Dave nor Jeannine knew how to express their anger in a healthy way. Growing up, they'd learned to be perennially polite and pleasant. Now, as they tried to assert their needs in the relationship, each had built up a lot of silent resentment toward the other. And their graciousness toward each other—clearly false—was only pissing off the other person more. Yet, they were too scared to come right out and say how they felt. I realized, in fact, that my insistent pushing to "get more honest" just might put me in the crosshairs of their rage.

With that, I quit pushing. Instead, over the next few sessions, I helped these two decide – quite politely – that they weren't ready to marry the other. When they left therapy, I was pretty sure these two would not make it down the aisle together. That was my hope, anyway, for their sakes. I was also very glad that I'd learned to use my mind/body as a diagnostic tool, rather than unwittingly provoke my clients' repressed anger. For everyone in the room that day, my mind/body had proved a trustworthy guide.

Letting it Flow

I once worked with Dennis, a middle-aged man who suffered from Crohn's disease, a chronic intestinal disorder. Other than feeling depressed, he was unable to recognize any other aspect of his emotional life. Everything he felt—anger, sadness, loneliness, and guilt—all ended up feeling like depression to him. His whole life felt flat and pointless.

One afternoon, Dennis walked into my office with an uncharacteristic smile on his face. He told me that as he was driving to my office, the motorist behind him had begun to loudly and repeatedly honk at him for going too slow. "I got angry," Dennis reported. "So I flipped him off!" Now, I don't customarily respond enthusiastically when a client behaves rudely, but in Dennis's case, his ability to feel and express something other than depression seemed like something to cheer about. "Congratulations!" I told him. He beamed.

After Dennis sat down, I asked him to close his eyes and sink into his body. Then I said, "See if you can find the part of you that responded by flipping the bird to the other driver." In past sessions, we'd tried this a few times—sinking into the body and trying to be aware of feelings or sensations—but Dennis hadn't been able to respond. So when he remained quiet for about 10 minutes, I began to think that, once again, this approach wasn't going to pan out.

Then Dennis opened his eyes. He told me he'd felt a very slight constriction in his throat and had asked himself what he would say if he could relax his throat and let the words come out. "Then suddenly, I saw and heard myself saying to that jerk, 'Screw you, I'm not going to do it your way!'" Dennis's face was alive with righteous indignation. "I'm tired of doing it the way everyone else wants it done!'"

In that moment, Dennis realized that for his whole life, he'd been accommodating others. "I've spent over 40 years as the ultimate "Yes Man", he said ruefully. Over the next several sessions, he talked about growing up with two hard-working, depressed parents who had taught their children not to burden them with their needs. Dennis had learned the lesson well. In fact, he'd learned that doing his chores and making life as easy as possible for his parents won him a modicum of respect, which counted for a lot in his affection-starved environment. Only when Dennis sank into his breath and down into his body could he retrieve that deeply-buried piece of himself—the part that was choking back his fury about always doing it "other people's way." The imagery experience opened the door for some very fruitful work and healing.

While most therapists are aware that repressed shame and guilt can lead to depression, we don't often conceptualize the problem as an energy blockage. But Dennis is a good example of what depressed energy looks like. Flat affect, listless energy, and all life seems very mundane. He is also a good example of the transformation that can occur when this energy gets moving. Face and eyes show signs of life, voice and expression more animated, and more hopeful about engaging life.

Certainly, there are many causes for depression, including genetic, environmental, and, of course, emotional. Dennis's depression may have stemmed from a number of factors, but regardless of the causes of a client's distress, the first order of business is to get their energy moving more freely. I still remember one of my first conversations with Master Lin, during which I explained what I did for a living and what psychotherapy looked like. To illustrate, I used an example of doing therapy with a depressed client. Before I had gotten very far, Master Lin asked me in bewilderment, "Why would you talk with someone who is depressed? Don't you know it is an energy problem in the body?" At the time, I had no idea what he was talking about. Now, through experience, I know that asking clients to sink into their body and to activate the energy through that process is usually more effective than merely talking about depression.

Slowing Down

While depression reflects one type of blocked energy, anxiety is another form of energy block. When someone is anxious, a lot of energy may be moving through the body but the flow is often jittery and erratic. In such cases, the simple act of slowing down, via focused breathing, can transform anxiety into awareness, thereby restoring a peaceful, balanced flow of energy.

Claire, a woman I worked with for about three years on anxiety issues, would sometimes catch me looking at the clock toward the end of the session. At some point, I noticed that when she saw me do this, her speech would begin to race as she tried to squeeze in everything she could before the session ended. When I brought this up to Claire, she tried to laugh it off, saying, "I'm just a time management freak." Then she stopped herself, looked away for a moment or two, and said softly, "You know, it does bother me."

"What do you think that's about?" I asked her. "Well, it probably is about time management in one way, as I never feel like I have enough time in here." She laughed, "We both know I could talk for three hours." I threw in my hunch. "I wonder if it's about not really getting to the heart of what you wanted to talk about in the session," I suggested. "Maybe you have talked so much that you haven't really said what you wanted to." We'd discussed before how Claire could fill up a lot of space with words but not really say what was important to her. As she reflected on this, I realized that once again I was doing my intellectual probing, hoping that our joint insight would somehow solve the mystery.

So I said, "Claire, why don't you close your eyes, sink into your breath and body, and imagine my looking at the clock. See what you notice." Claire sat quietly, breathing evenly for about two minutes. Then she opened her eyes and said, "Wow. I'm worried that you're going to dismiss me, throw me away—just like my mother did." As she finished speaking she drew a deep, shaky breath and exhaled with a long sigh that seemed to expel some deeply held repressed energy. Her entire body seemed more relaxed at the end of that breath. Slowing a client down, slowing myself down, and getting out of the way – sometimes it works just like it's supposed to.

Beyond the Story

Despite a therapist's beliefs and best intentions about mind/body wisdom, it can be very easy to get caught up in a client's words and story. That was my experience with Glenn, a wonderful guy and a very frustrating client. He had an anxiety disorder, coped with full-blown ADD, and was incredibly bright. None of those things frustrated me. What I found so frustrating about him was his niceness.

Glenn had made a career of being nice. He became especially nice when he wasn't feeling nice inside. Whenever he was disappointed, hurt or scared, and particularly when he was angry, he put on a mask of agreeable politeness. Glenn had tried hard his whole life to be the kind of man his mother and Catholic school teachers would be proud of – courteous, helpful, and considerate. Not surprisingly, Glenn didn't want to see himself as an angry man—even a justifiably angry one.

In session, I helped Glenn to understand why he often behaved so passive-aggressively with his wife and others. Just recently, for example, he'd agreed to come home a little earlier than normal after a long day teaching and go out to the movies with his wife. Then he arrived home 15 minutes too late to make the movie. It was a pattern, he would be overtly agreeable, then covertly resistant. As a college professor, Glenn warmed to the task of probing his behavior. He came to understand where he'd learned his life habits, and how and why they fueled his anxiety and undermined his important relationships. Because he was so perceptive and articulate in making these connections, it often left us both thinking he was making more progress than he really was.

Then, one day in session, Glenn was talking about how disrespectful his wife had been about the way he'd painted their bedroom. She'd sneered, "My six-year-old niece could do a better job than you, and she has." As he related this conversation, mimicking his wife, I heard the meanness in her tone. But Glenn laughed and said, "She was probably right." Then he laughed more heartily.

In the past, I would have asked him if he'd been angry about the incident, and he would have amiably agreed and continued on with his story. But on this particular day, I was able to stay calm and grounded and listen with another, more intuitive ear. As Glenn began to recount his wife's words of disdain, he began to breathe faster. Then, suddenly, he veered off on a tangential subject and began talking about how her family painted rooms together as a group; a few moments later, he then launched into a third story of a particular painting incident several years ago with her family.

Gently, I interrupted Glenn's wandering monologue. I asked him if he'd be willing to just sink into his body and breathe for a few moments. He looked slightly alarmed. "I can't see what that will accomplish," he said in a skeptical, professorial tone. "I can tell you whatever it is you need to know." But finally, he agreed to try.

Once he'd closed his eyes and was breathing deeply, I asked him return to the moment that his wife spoke disdainfully to him. "See if you can tell me again what happened, going slowly," I suggested. After continuing to breathe deeply for a few moments, Glenn told me once again what she'd said. "My six-year-old niece could do a better job than you. And she has." This time he said it quietly, weighing and reflecting on those words.

Rather than asking Glenn how he felt—to which he would have responded with a highly lucid and persuasive speech—I asked him several times if he was still in his body and in his breath. With his eyes still closed, he nodded. I wanted to give him the opportunity to track his responses with his body, and thereby ground himself in his physical being. When he'd finished telling me what his wife had said, I asked him what it felt like, at that moment, to be in his body.

Smiling a bit awkwardly, he said, "I have a burning in my belly." I asked him to breathe into that burning, and to ask himself what it was about. After a couple of moments, he smiled a little more. "I think it's my anger," he said. Another brief silence, followed by, "I think I'm mad as hell!" He was no longer smiling, and I heard more strength and congruency in his voice than I'd ever heard before.

Later, I realized that for a man like Glenn, talking was particularly unlikely to have much therapeutic impact. As an intellectual, Glenn was so habitually lost in his mind and analysis, and so disconnected from his here-and-now experience, that talk therapy only deepened the problem. Again, Johanson and Kurtz write, therapy too often "...tends to engage our minds alone, which are often overloaded, defended, and ruled by habitual responses. Analyzing and talking about our lives does not encourage contact with our core.... Experience is closer to our core than analysis—concrete, passionate, immediate felt experience."[3] Glenn needed no further understanding of his experience. What he needed—and thankfully got—was an immediate, felt experience of his deepest self.

A Couple's Heart

In couples work, I make frequent use of qigong techniques, just as I do with individuals. However, using mind/body approaches with couples requires an extra measure of awareness on the therapist's part. I learned this the hard way when I worked with Aaron and Vivian, a bright, articulate married couple who came to me to help them relate less hurtfully to each other. Vivian, a recovering alcoholic, tended to be incredibly sarcastic with Aaron. In response, he was often downright cruel. Each had already done a lot of work in individual therapy; in addition, Vivian regularly attended AA meetings and Aaron was active in Al-anon, but their relationship still bristled with anger and blame.

One evening in session, Vivian launched a caustic attack on Aaron's behavior with their 15-year-old daughter. "I can't believe you could talk to Marie like she's some idiot child. Do you really think that treating her like she's stupid is going to get her to pay attention to you? What the hell…." The words came out swiftly, drenched in disdain. Aaron visibly recoiled, as though he'd taken a punch. But he didn't look defeated; instead, he looked as though he was winding up to throw a punch right back.

I'd witnessed this destructive dance between them many times. This time, I stopped Vivian mid-sentence and asked her if she'd be willing to try to avoid their habitual loop and try something different. "You betcha," she immediately said, laughing a little in relief. So I asked her to breathe, sink into her body, and try to use her heart to remember other aspects of Aaron, the parts of him she enjoyed and loved. I asked her to remember why she married him. Then I asked her to recall times when she'd seen Aaron work hard to make the marriage a place where she felt cared about and respected.

I watched as Vivian's tightened jaw gradually relaxed, her wrinkled forehead softened, and her face began to change from angry to thoughtful and sad. In spite of myself, I was feeling quite proud of the way I'd intervened. When Vivian opened her eyes, she looked at Aaron with soft eyes. "I know I can be a bitch," she said contritely. "I think I feel so disconnected from you so often, and miss that connection, that I get cranky." Her face was open, almost pleading. "I'm sorry, Aaron," she said. "I want to do this differently."

Now I was feeling really good about my intervention. Just as I was imagining my clients concluding that I was one amazing therapist, Aaron exploded. "Goddamn it, Vivian, you should be sorry!" he yelled. "I'm sick and tired of your sarcastic bullshit and your haughty behavior. Who the hell do you think you are, talking to me like that?" When Vivian tried to speak, he waved away her words with a dismissive hand. "Apologies don't do it for me. I want you to stop it and stop it for good!"

After a shocked silence, we stumbled through the next few minutes to the end of the session. I wasn't quite sure what had just happened, but I tried my best to do a little damage control. As they got up to leave, Vivian shot me an angry look. In a quiet, cold voice, she said, "Don't you ever do that to me again."

Upon reflection, I realized that I'd made a serious mistake—I hadn't brought Aaron along on the guided imagery. I had helped Vivian disarm and become more vulnerable while leaving her husband loaded for bear. I have learned since then to do this exercise as a joint process. Even then, however, success is far from guaranteed. Often, by the time couples finally get to therapy, they have traveled so far down the road of hurt and resentment that they can no longer sink into their hearts, let go of their defensive anger, and remember their love and tenderness for each other. With these couples, I often just try to help them breathe, relax into their bodies, and unplug from their stress response and reactivity. I ask them to try to come from a place of personal integrity, so that they can behave with dignity in the relationship rather than resentment. Sometimes, the best I can do is to help a couple to part in a spirit of mutual respect and kindness.

Fortunately for Aaron and Vivian, they'd already done a lot of hard work on themselves. Vivian had completed a chemical dependency treatment program for her alcoholism; Aaron had participated in the family program; and both were working their 12 step programs and had done long term individual therapy. Furthermore, they were used to each other's hurtful behavior and had a tolerance for it that I'm not sure I could endure. Both felt they were in a better place in their relationship than ever before. So, a few sessions later, toward the end of a hard-working and productive hour, I asked them if they were interested in trying something new.

Looking at Vivian, I said with a playful grimace, "It involves breathing and sinking into your heart, but I think it might work a tad better than last time." We all laughed. "I sure hope so," she chuckled. I said, "The good news is that it's something you can carry home and use anywhere you want." After asking them to close their eyes, and sink into their bodies and hearts, I did a five-minute guided meditation on looking at the other person through their heart. I asked Vivian and Aaron to remember how wonderful the other had been in the early days of their relationship. I asked them to recall the original reasons they were attracted to, and had married, their partner.

Then I asked each of them to look at how much their partner had struggled over the years, and how much pain they had endured as they tried to stay connected to themselves and to each other. "Even though your partner may have hurt you many times," I said, "try to see how much they didn't want to do that, not ever, in their heart of hearts." As I spoke, I saw many emotions pass across Aaron and Vivian's faces – smiles of fond memories, grimaces of not-so-fond memories, traces of sadness.

"Now," I said softly, "having gone through so much with each other, see if you can find the love and goodness in each other's heart. Visualize the love and goodness that has never gone away. It has been certainly hard to find at times, but it has always been there." I continued to use reality-based imagery, acknowledging the hard times while emphasizing the good ones. I asked them to visualize a flower or a beautiful morning sun shining out of the other's heart, and to know the other's goodness would always be there, in their heart. "All you ever have to do to remind yourself of your partner's love and goodness," I said, "is to quiet yourself, close your eyes and look with your heart into your partner's heart."

Slowly, Aaron and Vivian opened their eyes. Tears splashed down Aaron's face as he reached both hands out to Vivian. "God, I love you," he said quietly. For a few moments, they held each other, weeping tears of love and grief. Tears rolled down my cheeks, too. It was one of those moments when you're working with two people who connect deeply with each other, right there in the moment, and you really wish you could just vanish and leave them to themselves. I quietly looked out my window, sank my consciousness into my breath, body and heart, and felt gratitude roll through my whole being.

CHAPTER 7:
ANYTHING BUT THAT!
HANDLING RESISTANCE TO
CHANGE

Usually, people come to therapy because they are suffering emotional pain that they can't resolve on their own. Some clients come into my office pretty clueless about what is causing their current difficulties. Others are admirably conscious of what is causing them problems and can articulate their issues with great clarity. But for the conscious and unconscious client alike, one thing is certain: They will resist change.

All of us—therapists and non-therapists alike—experience resistance to change. Think about promises you keep making to yourself to change your life—perhaps to start working out regularly, to eat more fruits and vegetables, to get to bed on time, or to stop watching so much TV. Many of us also vow repeatedly to change how we behave in our intimate relationships—we'll stop being so angry, passive, avoidant, and so on. We know what we want and even need to do, and at times we may be able to push through our resistance and take steps toward a different kind of behavior. But at other times, regardless of the depth of our desire to change, and regardless of the negative results of not changing, something inside us simply won't allow it.

Why We Love Ice Cream

The first and most challenging step is to fully face our own resistance. When we do so, we're usually presented with some dilemma that we're not yet ready to confront. For example, if we eat a lot of junk food or watch too much TV, it's often because some part of us feels that we need those things, that we deserve them, and simply cannot be deprived of them. Without regular infusions of sugar and sitcoms, we may start to experience an inner emptiness that is uncomfortable and perhaps even frightening.

As for the need to work out, well, if we faced that issue we might have to confront how badly we feel about our bodies and our overall health. Plus, as we go through our paces on the treadmill or elliptical machine, and if we are not watching TV or listening to the radio as we do so, we might even gain enough time and space to think about our lives—the bigger picture—which, in turn, may nudge us to become conscious of other life changes we might pursue. For most of us, it's a whole lot easier to sit in front of the TV with a bowl of ice cream on our laps than to take an honest, undistracted look at our lives.

In our intimate relationships, most of us can remember at some point planning to sit down with our partner to have a "big talk." Beforehand, we're pretty clear about what we want to say, what points we want to get across, and some idea about how we hope the talk will proceed. Then, afterward, we think to ourselves in bewilderment: "How was it that I didn't say what I really wanted to? Why did I back away?"

Part of the answer is that the familiar is usually more comfortable than the unknown—even when the familiar isn't serving us well. If we have to admit something about ourselves that we dislike or are ashamed of, or if we must look at something traumatic that happened to us in the past, it could be tough going for a while. Similarly, if we have to confront someone we love about something they dislike about themselves—and which may well make them angry with us— it's often easier to simply sidestep the turmoil. We're human, after all, and human beings have evolved to try to avoid pain and stay safe.

In hindsight, we may be able to see what we were resisting. We were avoiding dealing with something in ourselves, or in an intimate relationship, that would have challenged the status quo in some frightening way. The problem, of course, is that these vital, unraised issues only sink into the background of our lives, waiting to raise their ugly heads sometime in the future. But even when we know that, we often resist facing our tough issues in the here-and-now.

In therapy, it usually becomes clear pretty quickly that the client is going to have to wade into some pretty tumultuous waters. A client might need to make a behavior change, face some unhealthy dynamics in a relationship, or confront long-avoided emotional material. Whatever it is that needs facing, some part of the client will be reluctant to do so. Even though they have voluntarily walked into my office for help, I'm aware that some part of them would love to walk right out again. Just as sure as resistance will be part of the therapeutic process, facing that resistance will bring back our old friend, the stress response.

The Stress of Resistance

In graduate school, most therapists learn about the psychological function of resistance, and how to work with it primarily via talk, insight and emotional processing. But my qigong practice and training have helped me see that a major problem with resistance is that it triggers the stress response, which is a primarily physiological, rather than psychological, phenomenon. The body is saying, "No way am I going there," and yet we keep trying to use psychology to move it along.

Moreover, this resistance-triggered stress response may be going on right in the consulting room more often than we think. We know, of course, that the prospect of change can be stressful. We readily realize that when a client is contemplating some enormous life shift, such as leaving a marriage and facing the burdens of single parenthood, a stress response is practically par for the course. Likewise, if a client is confronting an unfaithful spouse, facing a person who once abused her, or doing an intervention with a loved one who is an active alcoholic, we would expect that person to be suffering significant stress.

What is less well understood is that at some point in therapy, the stress response gets activated in just about every client, even when they are talking about their issues with apparent calm and equanimity. A woman discussing the consequences of having been raised by an overly critical mother, or a man contemplating confronting his wife about her emotional distance, are likely to be suffering a stress response and its physiological manifestations in a therapy session. Some clients don't even need a specific topic—they're physiologically on "high alert" most of the time they're sitting in the chair across from you. After all, they're in therapy! Somewhere in their being, every client knows that significant change is in the air.

This is why insight alone rarely leads to significant change. Most of us can see what we should do, and many of us can even come to a deep understanding of why we're attached to a particular behavior. But the body, not the mind, is the primary vessel of the stress response. Understanding that physiology is an active player in resistance-induced stress can make working through resistance a much easier and less mysterious process.

Asking the Body What it Knows

The first practice I use is the simplest and often most powerful. I start with my usual approach, asking the client to breathe, relax, and sink into their body. But when I suspect they are resisting something, I also ask them to become aware of any internal sensations. If they notice something—perhaps a tight ball in their abdomen, tense shoulders, a nauseous feeling in their belly—it is often embarrassingly simple to help them move through it. It's embarrassing in the sense that in the past, when I recognized a client's resistance I would often end up analyzing it, sometimes processing it by getting the client to talk about it, or maybe educating them on resistance as a defense or trying another therapeutic approach entirely to sneak around their resistance. In hindsight, I often made things much more complicated than they needed to be.

Not long ago, I worked with a young couple, Daniel and Sheila, who were active in their synagogue and business community. Almost immediately, I noticed that Daniel would become very defensive in response to just about anything Sheila said that he perceived as critical. Because both of them put a lot of pressure on themselves to reach their life goals, I could see that stress might be part of their struggle. I could also see that some of Daniel's defensiveness seemed appropriate, since Sheila could get pretty angry and disparaging. At the same time, it was pretty clear to me that Sheila wanted to be more connected to Daniel.

In the midst of one session, Sheila asked Daniel to reflect on some recent behavior of his. He whipped around to face her, his face beet-red, his eyes like steel. Harshly, he asked: "Why is it that everyone else thinks I'm a perfectionist and you think I can't do anything right?" I intervened quickly, asking him to stop talking for a moment. He turned his steely gaze toward me, as though I were the next jerk who needed to be put in his place. "Daniel, I don't think this is about Sheila or about me," I said quietly. "See if you can just be quiet, breathe, and follow what's happening inside you."

Daniel closed his eyes. It took him a while to relax his body, but eventually he told me that he felt tightness across his arms and chest. I asked him to breathe into the tension. "Now I can feel the tension in my legs and butt," he said. So I asked him to breathe into that. Now he said he felt soft, mushy and queasy in his belly. "Yuck, I don't like that feeling!" he muttered. I asked him to breathe into that. After 3 or 4 minutes of doing so, Daniel's face slowly scrunched up, and with some difficulty he said, "I'm scared she'll walk right into my world and change everything about it, including me."

We all knew immediately who Daniel was talking about. During our initial session, he had talked about his mother in almost the same words. He'd said then, "My mother spent her life walking into mine, trying to change everything about me." Now, Daniel was in touch with his lifelong fear of being overwhelmed by his mother. "I think," he said softly, "that maybe some of this fear has gotten mixed up with the way I react to Sheila."

I asked Daniel to tell us more about that fear in relation to his mother, reminding him to stay with his breath and follow his internal sensations. He closed his eyes, took a few shallow breaths and then said, "It is hard to breathe and do this." He was quiet for a moment, and then added, "I think I didn't breathe around her so I'd take up as little space as possible, in hopes that she wouldn't say anything critical."

With a few words of guidance from me, Daniel tried to relax and breathe naturally again. But within a few moments, he began to shake his head back and forth. Then he opened his eyes. "The minute I imagine my mom, or you, Sheila, or even you, Patrick, giving me any kind of suggestion or feedback, I get queasy in my stomach and then my chest and arms want to explode outward," he said. "The only reaction I can imagine having to any comment from either of you is feeling pissed off." He paused and reflected for a moment, "Or, I guess I should say, scared." This moment of directly experiencing the source of his hair-trigger defensiveness opened a big door for Daniel to do some work on his resistance with Sheila, and on separating her out from his mother.

From my qigong perspective, I have learned to see resistance as an energy block. Something has gotten in the way of a person's ability to follow some emotional material and see where it will bring them. In the process, the natural flow of their energy gets diverted, or even shut down. A key step in unblocking this dammed-up energy is simply giving ourselves the time and silence to notice the bodily sensations that attend this blockage. As noted trauma expert Peter Levine writes in Waking the Tiger, "Once you become aware of them, internal sensations almost always transform into something else. Any change of this sort is usually moving in the direction of a free flow of energy and vitality."[1]

A free flow of energy and vitality—isn't that what we all want? What Daniel and Sheila like about this simple technique is that it is so portable; once you learn it, you can practice it any time, anywhere. Once Daniel and Sheila had used the technique several times in session, they'd developed enough mutual trust to use it at home, especially when they felt stuck in some familiar argument that was going nowhere. Gradually, the process began to free up this couple's resistant and defensive energy and to bring some vitality directly into their discussions.

Getting Unstuck

Many of us to try to keep our resistance in place with self-judgments and dictates to "keep a stiff upper lip." Take Sam. At the age of 46, he'd come to see me for help with depression. After a few months in therapy, he began to talk about the physical abuse he'd received at the hands of his father, something he'd never told anyone about. He told me that his dad, an ex-football player, had wanted his only son to be "tough," which he'd tried to foster by relentlessly bullying and occasionally beating Sam.

My client had been describing his father's violence for about 10 minutes, initially in a very detached, objective tone. But the longer Sam spoke, the more personal and emotional his language became. "My dad would beat me—his son—just to prove how tough he was," he said in a voice bitter with anguish. "God, how could he do that?"

Then, without warning, Sam's body became very fidgety and he looked away from me. When I asked him what was happening, he said in a very mocking voice, "I sound like a fucking, self-pitying baby." Having worked with abuse survivors for over 25 years, I could see a number of ways to go with what Sam had just said. In the past, I might have done some pyschoeducation with him around shame and how it is always part of recovering from childhood trauma. Or I might have told him that his anger was probably misdirected toward himself, and that he should try to get in touch with his anger toward his father. But I chose something else.

For a long time, I've believed that "self-pity" has gotten an unfairly bad name for itself. Generally, I view it as an arrow pointing to something vital that needs attention. I had worked with Sam long enough that he knew my style and had a significant amount of trust in me. So after talking with him a bit about the self-pity he felt and how appropriate I believed it was, I said I thought it was pointing us to something very important. I explained to Sam that his self-judgment was getting in the way of something that needed healing. I asked him if he felt able to breathe into his self-pity to understand it better.

Nodding, he closed his eyes. Within two minutes, Sam was sobbing—that kind of raw, aching sob that is so unmistakably genuine, so present, and so healing. Sitting forward on the couch, elbows on his knees, hands over his face, his body relaxed into his grief as he allowed his compassion for himself, and my care for him, to hold him in a way he'd needed to be held for a long time. He simply let himself go with the waves of grief, just letting his body do what it had needed to do since he was a child. When he finished crying and had wiped away his tears, Sam's face had both a softness and an aliveness, neither of which had ever been present before.

Sam was directly experiencing what we all need to learn—that our feelings are just part of life. That doesn't mean we need to understand and process every last one of them. Certainly, some people rely too much on their unfettered feelings to navigate life, which can cause as many problems as fleeing from them. Attachment and avoidance are simply different kinds of "stuckness." The Buddhists, like the Taoists, would say, "don't resist it or cling to it." As Sam discovered, permitting his feelings to move through his body allowed them the space they'd long needed. Generally, once our feelings get their "say," they're ready to move on and out of our body, restoring us to renewed calm and vitality.

The Pain of Change

Nonetheless, the prospect of facing our deepest feelings can be daunting. For several months I'd been working with Eleanor, a 36-year-old woman who'd come into therapy to get help with her anxiety. Her husband, Jeff, suffered from long-standing and severe depression and anger problems, yet he had steadfastly refused to get help. The couple's social life was threadbare and their intimacy and lovemaking was nonexistent.

Eleanor was struggling with a wrenching decision: Should she stay in her 15-year marriage and create an independent life for herself and her two daughters, or walk out, take the kids, and let Jeff fend for himself? For years, she'd told herself that her marital problems were "just temporary" and that surely "something would change" for Jeff and, by extension, for their marriage and family. In my office, Eleanor was struggling to pull her head out of the sand and face her actual situation.

On the way to therapy one morning, she heard a radio report about how some adults respond to the midlife transition with major depression. Listening intently, she began to wonder whether this was what her husband was going through. Maybe Jeff was stuck in a deep midlife crisis (even though his slide into depression had started in his mid 20s) that he simply couldn't pull himself out of. Maybe she was being too judgmental of him—heck, maybe she was in a midlife crisis herself! By the time Eleanor had gotten to my office, her anxieties about her looming marital decision were running rampant. Was she making too big a deal out of this? Was therapy making a problem in her marriage where there really wasn't one? Was it possible that *she*, in fact, was the problem?

Listening to Eleanor, I suspected that the radio report had brought up in her a deep longing—the longing for a more normal and comforting marriage, in which you trooped through life transitions with your partner, loyally hung in there, and eventually worked things through. I knew that a major ongoing struggle for Eleanor was her denial of her husband's condition and its consequences for her and her children, both now and for the foreseeable future. She had used the defense of magical thinking for some time – "If I don't think it's as bad as it is, then it's *not* that bad!" I guessed that the radio report had slammed her full force back into her denial and had re-triggered her longing to find a rational, acceptable answer to Jeff's unwavering refusal to get help.

In the past, I would have tried a more cognitive therapeutic approach to Eleanor's resurgent resistance to facing her family situation. I might have gently confronted her denial and reminded her how often it had been difficult for her to face the realities of her married life. Or perhaps I would have tried to convince her by holding up all of the evidence she'd shared with me of Jeff's severe depression, his refusal to get help, and its consequences to her and her daughters. Instead, I merely suggested that she breathe quietly, sink into herself, and ask herself what the radio report had brought up for her that was so difficult.

After sitting a couple of minutes with her eyes closed, Eleanor slowly clutched both hands to her heart. Her face had become drawn and sad. When she opened her eyes, they were brimming with tears. "My heart just aches," she said quietly. "I'm afraid I may never know what love feels like again." When I'm working with someone in therapy, I don't often think to myself, "I'm glad I'm not in the situation my client is in," but at that moment, I did. The pain in Eleanor's voice, and in her eyes, seemed to cut bone-deep.

I saw Eleanor only a couple of times after that. She told me that she didn't need any more sessions because her anxiety had diminished and she now knew what she had to do. "What I need is to find courage, and I'm not going to find that in therapy," she told me. I'm not really sure why she left, but when she told me she said it with such clarity and firmness, I knew to get out of her way and let her follow the course that seemed right for her. But what I do know is that her experience in therapy had moved her closer to her real experience of life, especially her life with Jeff. I could only hope it would be helpful to her.

The Resistance to Longing

Among the biggest issues we resist facing in therapy is one that doesn't get named very clearly. It is our longing–a longing for love, affection, approval, validation, and affirmation. In our consumer-driven quest for material rewards in Western culture, many people are significantly deprived of the caring and acceptance from others that they yearn for. We often get mislead into believing what we need to feel good about ourselves is "things" rather than caring relationships. I usually try to avoid using the term "needs" because being "needy" is so often used pejoratively in our society. Nonetheless, all of us need a certain level of care and validation in our lives, and without it, we pay a price. I believe that if we could measure the physical and emotional health costs of unmet longing, it would be staggering.

Given the vulnerability that many of us feel when exposing our deep needs to another, it's easy to understand why we resist and avoid facing them—even in therapy. Regardless of a client's intellectual understanding of the issue, this longing for care is often one of the hardest areas to get in touch with, and to accept, as part of one's true nature. So deep is our resistance to this vulnerability that even breath work can run into stiff resistance.

I had been working with Eric for about three years around his struggle to find intimacy and the deep ache he felt at its absence in his life. He was married, but his marriage had lacked closeness beyond the early months of courtship, when intimacy and sex had been almost indistinguishable. Eric knew that making love made it easier for him for respond to his longing for touch and affection, but given his wife's vastly decreased interest in sex, he had no idea how to ask for, or experience, her care for him.

He understood how his childhood had shaped his fear of this longing, for he'd been raised by two Scandinavian, shame-based parents who had rarely been able to show him warmth and care. But months of talking about this in therapy, and even Eric's occasional ability to feel sad or angry about his childhood deprivation, had little impact on how he responded to his wife or on the painful, echoing emptiness he felt inside.

One afternoon, Eric came in my office with an uncharacteristic spring in his step. He was excited to tell me how well his recent evaluation at work had gone. (Excited for a Scandinavian, that is.) About three sentences into sharing his good news, Eric abruptly lost track of what he was saying and brought the story to a quick close. When I asked him what had just happened, he said, "I have no idea." I asked him to begin breathing and sinking into his body to see if he could let his body help him find out.

We had tried this process a few times before, so Eric knew he was looking for his breath to open up something that might not be available to his thinking brain. He closed his eyes, relaxed, sank his breath into his body, and sat like that for about 30 seconds. Then he opened his eyes and laughed nervously. "I can't breathe," he said. "Let me try it again."

Thirty seconds later, he opened his eyes again. "No breath, and totally black. Wow. Something powerful must be going on." He closed his eyes once again, and after about a minute, he opened them and shook his head. "I can't believe how shallow my breathing gets," he said, trying to smile but looking increasingly uncertain. "I don't know what's going on."

I had a hunch. "Eric, I have a feeling that what's happening for you has something to do with me," I said. "Something about how you came in here and what you were sharing with me. Do you want to try sinking into your body again while I coach you through it?"

Continuing to look puzzled and unsure, Eric agreed. For the fourth time, he closed his eyes and relaxed into his body, while I recounted what had happened when he'd first walked into my office. I told him that he'd come in more excited than I'd ever seen him before, bursting to share something with me that he seemed very proud of. But then, I said, when he'd started to share his excitement and saw *my* enthusiasm for him, he'd totally lost what he was talking about. At that point, I told him, his face had changed abruptly, from animated and pleased to somewhere between sad and tense.

After a few more quiet moments, Eric opened his eyes. For a little while after that, he stared at the large plant next to me. Then, finally, he said in a quiet, stunned voice: "Wow. I just had this image of being a little boy and wanting to crawl in your lap." He glanced at me and then turned away. "I wanted you to hug me and be proud of me." He seemed shocked by this image of uncontestable longing. He looked at me again, seemingly from miles away. Then, refocusing on me and on the resonance of what he'd just said, he looked sad, embarrassed, and very vulnerable, like a deer caught in headlights. He turned away again.

I leaned forward in my chair, smiled warmly and said, "That is a beautiful image Eric, because that's just how I feel. I would love to scoop up that little boy and hold him as long as he wanted to be held. I do feel happy, and even proud of you." I felt a little embarrassed myself at expressing my feelings so directly, but I don't think he noticed. Eric was now looking down at the floor, a couple of tears on his cheeks and a relaxed smile of mingled happiness and sadness on his face.

My experience with Eric, as well as with other clients, has taught me to be more present myself and to try to flexibly respond to what's needed in the moment. However simple and effective it can be at times, telling a client to "just breathe" sometimes doesn't work—at least not initially. For Eric, breathing into his body had begun to jostle open a door into his unconscious that was too big and frightening for him to pass through alone. So I went along with him, guiding him with my voice and care, and letting him know I was accompanying him on the journey.

At other times, asking a client to breathe into his or her body— even with close support and guidance—may not bear fruit. In my experience, this is usually because the client is harboring some intense longing that he or she isn't yet ready to face. Then, I do use the good hard work of conventional therapy, building up trust and gradually introducing breathing and imagery when the moment seems right.

Looking for the Longing

Getting to the heart of our resistance may feel like a bewildering journey at times—what is it, exactly, that we're resisting in the first place? In the arena of intimate relationships, especially, I've found that when clients run into strong resistance, it's usually about a longing for something they can't quite name. It may be a longing for a show of affection, for some recognition, for an apology, or just a yearning to be fully met and cared about.

At other times, the longing can be about wanting one's love and care to be accepted by another. I believe that our longing to be loved is matched by our longing to love and care for others, so that when our love isn't received, it can cause deep pain. This is often hard to name because by the time people get into therapy, their anger and resentment toward the person who has spurned their love is often paramount, and they resist returning to an openhearted place.

What makes it so challenging to reach this deep place of longing is that resistance does its job so well, deftly covering up our deepest feelings about significant others with safer and more tolerable responses, such as anger, blame or indifference. So, I would like to offer a modest proposal. If you find yourself embroiled in repeated struggles with an important person in your life that you can't seem to get clarity about, go sit somewhere, close your eyes and sink into your breath for a few moments. If you notice any physical sensations, sink into those. Now, ask yourself, "What am I longing for from this person?" This gentle inquiry may not provide you with the whole answer, or provide it right away. But listen carefully. You may discover something about yourself, and your relationship, that points the way toward deep healing.

CHAPTER 8:
HEALING TRAUMA

The theme of this book, "You can do so much by doing so little," holds powerfully true for working with trauma. The simple, Taoist-based practices of breathing and imagery can be effective tools to help free up energy blocked by trauma. While I make no claim to being a trauma expert, I have worked with traumatized individuals for 30 years and have found these techniques to facilitate the healing process in deep and sometimes surprising ways.

When I teach therapists about using qigong approaches in trauma work, I'm often asked to explain more about "how" to use breathing, imagery and energy work with clients. Invariably, some therapists are disappointed that they don't leave my class with some specific, detailed protocol. But when clinicians ask for more "how to," I think that many are really asking how I can help them relieve their own understandable anxieties about working with trauma survivors. My response: by breathing, using imagery, and tracking your own energy. In my own experience, utilizing qigong concepts and practices on myself, as well as with the client, makes the process of working with trauma much easier for everyone in the room.

Trauma as an Energy Blockage

Traumatic memory is probably the clearest expression of an emotional problem as an energy blockage. When children are abused, they instinctively shut a door on their natural responses to the trauma in order to survive. All of the physiological and emotional energies that the body needs to discharge—the energies of terror, grief, anger, and other trauma responses—are immediately repressed. It's a critical, sometimes life-saving coping skill, but it comes with a steep price. The survival-driven repression of this vital energy can significantly hinder a person's emotional life in adulthood, especially the establishment of intimate relationships that require, by definition, access to one's feelings.

Understanding trauma as an energy blockage has been a turning point in my work with trauma survivors, allowing me to work far more effectively than I had in the past. Like many therapists, I tried to help survivors by encouraging them to talk and work through their feelings around their trauma. This process was certainly helpful, as it offered my clients a safe relationship and place to finally experience their long-buried feelings. But this way of working was usually slow and often led to incomplete healing for the client. I didn't know, then, that I had missed a key element in trauma and its healing—the body. Both the repository of trapped energy and the source of its renewal, the body is our most powerful ally in trauma healing.

As I have said, I deeply respect the power of talk therapy. It is simply that it is often not enough, especially in the realm of trauma work. By virtue of its emphasis on thought and argument, by poking around trying to decide which door to open and which clues to follow in ones' psyche, straight talk therapy tends to provoke a person's natural defensiveness. Initially, this can be useful as it allows the client to understand where they are headed in their therapy work and how powerful the issues are they are going toward. But once that resistance is in full swing, our only way of working with it is via more talk, insight-seeking, and trying to help people feel their way through their "therapeutic blocks."

By contrast, body-based processes such as imagery and focused breathing allow us to dive deep below our defensive structures. As Belleruth Naparstek eloquently writes in Invisible Heroes, "imagery sidesteps the logical and analytic centers of the brain. It is a useful way to slip around psychological resistance, fear, hopelessness, worry and doubt and grab a foothold on attitude and self-esteem before the more literal, logical thinking mind, with all its worrying monologue, can even get wind of its presence and start arguing with it."[1] Together, imagery and breathing not only soften this resistance, but also help clients to deactivate the stress response and take hold of powerful tools to navigate their lives, both in and out of therapy.

One Angry Guy

A recent client, Derrick, was a successful cardiologist who had been "advised" by his hospital administration to seek counseling after enough nurses had complained about his episodic angry outbursts with staff. Normally a charming man and a very competent physician, he had a long history of blowing up when certain stressors pushed him over the edge. Too many critically ill patients needing immediate care, the occasional deaths of one of his patients, and the ongoing stressors of budget cuts effecting his clinic combined to make him chronically tense and vulnerable to explosions of rage.

In our first session, Derrick admitted that he had a temper and could "really lose it when my buttons get pushed." Toward the end of the hour, he mentioned that his father had been physically abusive with him and his brother. "I suppose I should work on that," he added quickly, "but I just want to get my anger under control this round. Maybe I'll come back another time to look at the other stuff."

In other words, Derrick was telling me that he was in therapy only because he'd been pushed into it and wanted only enough therapy to stop his offensive behavior. Not that uncommon. Many people come into therapy at the behest of others. I told him, "Coming to therapy is like going to your doctor. We'll first work on what is acutely hurting you. Down the road, I may give you advice about possible chronic issues that affect your life. But right now, let's deal with the pain that got you in my door." He smiled at my medical analogy.

As Derrick came to trust that I wasn't an agent of his clinic or out to push him in a direction he didn't want to go, he began to talk about how his anger also affected his marriage and his treatment of his three school-aged children. He could be short and irritable when he brought work stress home, especially when he felt incapable of attending to his family's needs. When he was moody, they walked on eggshells around him, and two of his kids had begun to avoid him altogether. While it was clear that Derrick loved his family, it became equally clear, both to him and me, that his unpredictable outbursts were hurting everyone around him.

During the next five months, Derrick did some good work around understanding the situations that pushed his buttons, looking at how he tried to control situations that were beyond his control, and getting in touch with remorse about the people he had hurt. He knew that his father's abuse had something to do with his explosive anger, but he felt committed to taking responsibility for his behavior and not blaming it on his dad. I didn't push it. We began to talk about terminating therapy.

Then, late one afternoon, Derrick walked into my office looking like he hadn't slept all night. "I feel like a black cloud is following me," he said in a low, tight voice. "There is a constant pit in my stomach. It feels like it has to do with my father." He looked down, clenching and unclenching his fists. "I don't want to walk into that crap. I feel sick even thinking about it."

Opening Up

I knew that I needed to respond to Derrick's admission with great care and respect. For most people, the journey of healing from trauma, of opening that long-closed door, is undertaken with great trepidation. An individual who has been abused instinctively knows that behind that closed door are not just memories, but an enormous storehouse of energy, both physical and emotional. If the door is opened too wide or too quickly, the sudden release of trapped energy can trigger an overwhelming flood of emotions, a feeling of being out of control, and excessive vulnerability. But, if approached carefully, energy work can do much to free a survivor from the invisible chains of trauma and release a much fuller capacity to be human.

Assessing the clients' readiness to begin trauma healing is crucial. Some clients, especially those with post-traumatic stress disorder, come into therapy with their abuse issues leaking out into their lives; it's very clear to them that they need to face those issues. Other clients come in aware of unresolved trauma and have simply "had enough" of the different ways it has diminished their life. For still others, awareness of trauma may come up for the first time during therapy. Sometimes, a client is ready to work immediately on the memory aspect of the abuse; other times, as in Derrick's case, it is important to address other issues until the client is ready. While he had initially indicated that he wasn't ready to work on his abuse, the fact that he'd now allowed the symptoms to show up in his body, and had reported them to me, were the cues I needed to determine that it was time.

When a client indicates that he or she is prepared to begin working on memories of abuse, I usually spend a little time introducing the concept of blocked energy. I often call up the image of a door, describing how the client's natural, healthy energy is trapped behind that closed, locked door. I then explain that at the time of the abuse, the client's body was not able to process all of its natural responses because it had frozen into a survival mode. As trauma specialist, Peter Levine, writes in Waking the Tiger, "My observation of scores of traumatized people has led me to conclude that post-traumatic symptoms are, fundamentally, incomplete physiological responses suspended in fear." [2]

I then explain to my client that following a trauma, a person's body often stays stuck in the freeze mode—for years or decades. A traumatized individual needs to unfreeze his or her physiology and emotions in order to complete the natural response that wasn't possible in the moment of trauma. I will say to my client, "Your task is simply to stay present to yourself, stay connected to me, and let your body finish what it has wanted to do for a long time."

The Embodied Breath

When I work with a trauma survivor, the way I use breathing is similar to the way I use it with other clients—with a major caveat. Breathing and becoming embodied can trigger a very direct connection with past abuse. So I always caution trauma survivors that the kind of breathing I would like to teach them will sink them down into their bodies and the sensations they find there. This process, I say, may connect them with the feelings or memories of the abuse more quickly than they are ready for.

In my experience, this sudden connection rarely leads to anything more detrimental than some very short-term emotional unplugging or dissociating. When this happens, it sometimes looks as though somebody flipped a switch, whereby a client who may have started crying suddenly freezes up and feels nothing. Usually, a little reconnection with me or themselves, via asking them to breathe, look at me, and remember what they are doing and who I am, helps them to sink back into the healing process. Subsequently, they're usually able to monitor how deeply their breath takes them into their emotions. As I explain these possible responses to my client, my intent is to provide both reassurance and a realistic framework for the experience.

I also let my client know that throughout the process, I will help them to stay safe by reminding them to stay connected to their bodies. I have learned that it's very important to ask clients to stay connected to bodily sensations, and not just allow them to "have feelings" about the trauma. As Maryanna Eckberg writes in *The Body in Psychology*, "Grounding the telling of the trauma story in sensation keeps the survivor connected to the present reality and to the therapist and results in a natural pacing in which the client leads, sets the pace, and is in control of the process."[3]

So, if I notice that a client has begun to breathe shallowly, I will ask them to come back to their breath and deepen it. If they start to dissociate or get overwhelmed at any point in the process, I will ask them to focus on their tight chest, knotted-up stomach, or whatever physical sensation they're conscious of. This experience of moment-to-moment bodily awareness will usher them safely back to the here and now.

Shedding Expectations

Years ago, when a client expressed readiness to work on a traumatic history, I had a loose but fairly clear sense of how the process should go. Based on my training and experience, I followed a protocol that roughly included cautioning the client that this work could last for quite some time; that they should set up a strong support network outside of my office; and that we would talk about the intricacies of contacting me between sessions, should the need arise. I would talk about the possible emotional flooding they might experience, nightmares, relationship difficulties, and other problems that may arise during trauma work.

Now, using my Taoist and qigong understanding, I have no expectations of what should happen, or how. My job is to get my mind—my assumptions, rules, goals and hopes—out of the way. I tell my client, too, that there is nothing specific they need to look for or go after. Instead, I encourage them to just respond to what comes up in the process of sitting quietly and allowing their body to do what it wants to.

While feelings are not the goal, I tell my clients that certain feelings may well be part of what their body wants to let go of. I encourage them to simply allow the natural process that was stopped to finish its cycle. I suggest that they use as little effort as possible, trusting their breath, their body, and our relationship to do the rest. I also tell them that I will respond to whatever comes up, that I have been down this road many times with clients, and that if we both stay present to the process, it will show us how to be.

Derrick: A Boy's Sorrow

By the time Derrick had walked into our session "with a pit in my stomach," he had already done some breath work in therapy. He had even had bought some breathing and relaxation CDs off the Internet and was using them sporadically. Breath work had helped him to moderate his stress, and consequently his anger, on many occasions. For example, when he walked into his house at the end of a high-stress day at the clinic and could feel everyone "coming at me, hell bent for election with all their needs," he'd learned to say, "Give me 10 minutes to catch my breath and I'd be glad to listen." His wife and kids quickly understood that this request for downtime would benefit everyone, and gladly gave him some quiet time to unwind.

But now, I told Derrick, if he was willing, we could go deeper with the breath work. We could use it to help begin to address, and move past, the history that so hounded him. When he indicated that he was ready to work with his memories, I asked him to do nothing more than just sink into his body and the sensation that was haunting him—that hollow, sickening pit in his stomach. "Just try to stay with your breath," I said, "and try to stay with me."

Derrick closed his eyes and began to breathe. For a few moments, the room was quiet. Then, Derrick buried his face in his hands and a sob escaped him. For the next 20 minutes, he poured out stories of his father's cruelty towards him and his brother, often weeping as he spoke. "First, he'd corner one or both of us and kind of toy with us a while, slapping us softly, and laughing as we flinched. He'd have this big smirk on his face, and then, without any warning, he'd just haul off and start beating one of us," Derrick gasped between sobs. "We never knew which one of us was going to get it the worst until the blows started landing."

As I listened, I kept reminding Derrick to breathe. Knowing how deeply and directly he was contacting his past, I also asked him repeatedly if he was staying connected to me and to the here-and-now. He would usually nod, continuing to cry and talk. Then, all at once, the process took a common, and sad, turn. In an anguished voice, Derrick began to cry out, "I know I was a bad boy!" and, "I'm sorry I made you so mad!"

I was not surprised by Derrick's abrupt shift. At some point, nearly all childhood abuse survivors run into some shame, self hate, and/or a strong feeling that they were somehow responsible for the abuse they suffered. It is a predictable response because in most cases, self-blame was a major psychological defense used by the child to cope with the abuser's betrayal. In my experience, it must be addressed promptly so that it does not get in the way of the healing process.

Quickly, I asked Derrick to come back to the present and be in his breath and in the room with me. As he opened his eyes, I briefly explained what I believed was happening regarding his sudden attack of self-blame. Then, I gently returned him to a crucial, healing image of himself that he had remembered in one of our earlier sessions.

The Boy in the Tree

In that earlier session, I had encouraged Derrick to access some reality-based imagery from his early life that he might use to counter the self-loathing he felt about hurting his family with his explosive anger. With a few guided imagery instructions from me, Derrick closed his eyes and soon found himself with his brother in a tree fort in a big, leafy oak tree out back behind his childhood home. It was the fort where he and his brother had often retreated as kids to play, relax, and escape from brewing trouble.

As I encouraged Derrick to fully imagine the experience—the feel of the rough wooden boards underneath him, the twittering sounds of birdsong—he recalled a moment in his childhood when he had sat perched in the tree fort and happened to look up into the sky. Gazing at the peaceful, enveloping expanse of blue, he'd known at that moment that there was a goodness in him, and a goodness in the world, that was untainted by his father's abuse. "It's the only time I ever remember experiencing a truly spiritual feeling," he'd told me quietly.

Again and again, I have found that using imagery along with breath work changes the entire process of working with trauma. While imagery experiences can be intense, they can also elicit a strong sense of personal power. As Naparstek explains

> Imagery...restores mastery and control by providing an instantaneously effective way to soothe and calm an overwrought psyche. People often compare it to finding a different channel with a radio tuner, coming upon a mellow frequency that had not been perceived but apparently had always been there. They are relieved and gratified to discover they can teach themselves to turn away from their intense agitation and enter a state of peacefulness in a matter of seconds.[4]

Now, as I watched Derrick struggle once again with self-blame—this time about having "caused" his father's abuse—I asked him whether he could hook up the kid who'd just been beaten to the kid in the tree fort, the kid with the undeniable goodness. He closed his eyes and took a few deep, quiet breaths. Then his face contorted into one of the most sorrowful looks I had ever seen. He began to sob deeply, rocking back and forth and moaning, "I was so scared, I was so scared." As I sat with Derrick, witnessing the raw pain that exploded from being in touch with his goodness at the same time he was in touch with being abused, I felt tears fall down my own cheeks.

As our session drew to a close, Derrick looked spent, but calm. Years ago, before I used breath work, I would have told Derrick that he'd probably be on an emotional roller coaster for the next few weeks, and I would have laid out some coping strategies to deal with the expected upheaval. Instead, I told him not to expect anything in particular. "Just try and be present to whatever comes to you," I advised. Taking a deep breath, he nodded.

I reminded Derrick that I had no idea where this process would continue to take him, but that his body would reliably show him where he needed to go. It was possible, I said, that he might not have to do further work on his abuse. But if he did— if his body got that haunted feeling again—he would only have to do as much as his body needed him to do. I also let him know that if any uncomfortable feelings came to him between sessions, he could breathe into them but move past them into the bigger Derrick, into the here-and-now, and tell himself he would deal with the memories when he got to my office.

Once again, my chief job was to trust Derrick's process. As Greg Johanson and Ron Kurtz write in *Grace Unfolding: Psychotherapy in the Spirit of the Taoteching*, "When a therapist has no investment in changing anybody, looking good as a therapist, or some other personal agenda, she can be open to (the client's) reality and allow it to wash over her without prejudice or defense."[5] Derrick would experience the process his body and psyche needed, not one influenced by my ideas or protocols. I now believe that in the past, one of the reasons my clients encountered so many of the consequences I outlined in my prep work with them was because I suggested that they would have them. Derrick was free of my ideas and free to be with the process his experience needed him to have.

When Derrick came in the following week, he exuded a kind of quiet, calm energy. He said that he'd felt very sad for a couple of days after the last session, but also that he'd been able to hold onto his goodness in the midst of his grief. "You know, I was surprised at how good I felt as the week went on, and how good I felt about myself." He said this with a soft, peaceful smile. He said he'd also felt very relieved that he wasn't expected to dredge up and relive every horrible moment of the abuse and anguish he'd lived through.

The abuse issues did come back, twice more. Specific memories simply floated into Derrick's body consciousness, leaving him with the familiar pit in his stomach. Both times, by breathing into this bodily sensation and accompanying emotions, he was able to handle his discomfort until he saw me again. In session, using the same process as before, he worked with the bodily sensations, emotions and memories of abuse. Afterward, the memories seemed to lose their primal power. Derrick could now contemplate them reasonably calmly, feeling some sadness for the small boy within him, but without the accompanying terror and deep grief. For the next couple of months, he continued to work on current issues, mostly around becoming more vulnerable in his relationship with his wife.

By the time Derrick left therapy, he felt more grounded and better able to be intimate with his wife and kids. "Sometimes, I realize I'm even happy," he said, a note of wonder in his voice. How much these shifts had to do with working on his abuse issues, specifically, we will never know. Was his abuse work thorough enough? Time will tell. What was clear, though, was that the work Derrick did on his past was all he needed to do at the time. He knew that he could always return for more exploration and support. For the moment, we trusted his body's continuing guidance, trusted his commitment to be present to himself, and trusted that he would continue to bring "right effort" to his current life. For now, it seemed like more than enough.

SECTION 3:
BEYOND THE SELF

CHAPTER 9:
A HEART-CENTERED LIFE

When a person finds the Way, heaven is gentle.
When the Way is not found, earth is harsh.[1]

So, what do you get when you learn to breathe naturally on a regular basis, use healing imagery throughout your day, and organize the world around you so that it radiates positive and peaceful energy? What do you get when you're able to monitor your stress response so that it turns on only when absolutely essential? And what do you get when you're able to maintain a physiological and neurological equilibrium throughout the day that contributes to a general sense of well-being? What you get is the capacity to live with an open heart.

This open heart is not just another name for our emotional heart. It is partly that, but it's also bigger than that. In the qigong tradition, it's what we call "heart energy," and it refers to the spirit. But we need to be careful here because what is meant by that word in the East is generally very different then what we mean in the West. Here in the West, "spirit" gets interpreted in many different ways by many different belief systems, and the very existence of spirit is widely debated. In the East, the spirit is viewed as undeniable, something that comes with the package of your humanity. It lives inside of you; it is the source of your innate goodness. If you have a mind and a body, by definition you have a spirit.

In qigong, as in many Eastern spiritual practices, the natural outcome of a conscious mind/body practice is a more open heart. In Taoist understanding, when your mind and body are in balance, when you are grounded in your original nature, and when you continue to cultivate your energy through regular practice, your heart energy has no choice but to open. It is simply in the nature of things.

Master Lin and I call this phenomenon "the mind/body/heart approach to health and life." We believe it is a more culturally accurate way to describe the concept of "spirit," and it sidesteps all of the confusion around the term. When I use this paradigm to think about therapy, I am reminded that the goal of therapy isn't only to be healed, but transformed. In the past, my clients too often left therapy using their emotions not just as a guide to sorting themselves out, but also as the major orienting principle of their lives. Too often, they left with a clear sense of their own personal boundaries and needs, but without knowing much about how to care for others, or how to feel more connected to the world at large. And the person most responsible for those failures was me. I didn't know how to help my clients do anything else.

Before we can truly care for others, of course, it helps to love ourselves. I believe that, by and large, psychotherapy does a poor job of helping people feel significantly better about themselves on this particular issue. We help clients uncover why they don't love themselves and to become more accepting and compassionate about why they don't feel good about themselves. But traditional psychotherapy rarely ends with clients experiencing authentic self-love. I cringe to think of all the times I sat with clients who believed themselves to be unlovable, urging them on to discover ways to see the good in themselves and to "work on" loving themselves. I remember my clients nodding politely as their eyes glazed over.

But once again, my qigong practice has helped me find a way to help clients significantly change their relationship with themselves. I now use a simple practice that gets to the heart of healing and transformation much more quickly and directly than all of the psychic digging and sorting I used to do. It's as simple as helping a person remember a time when they were aware of, and directly experienced, their innate, undeniable goodness.

One of my favorite Spring Forest Qigong healing meditations is visualizing oneself as an eight-year-old, running on beautiful green grass with bright flowers and calm waters all around and a beautiful blue sky overhead. You are encouraged to feel your healthy body, your vital energy and your open and loving heart. Then, you're invited to sense your goodness so fully that you are filled with love, kindness and forgiveness.[2] In part, this is a powerful meditation for me because I did a lot of running at that age, just for the pure thrill of it. That meditation is based in reality for me, and it brings me joy and openheartedness.

A Memory of Goodness

I ask most of my clients if they have a memory of being in touch with their goodness. I ask if they can remember a moment when they simply knew that they were perfectly fine just the way they were. I've had clients remember riding their bicycles down sunny country roads, taking a running leap off the dock of a summer cabin, walking onto the baseball field at the beginning of summer vacation, or sitting on the front porch with their grandmother. Most people call up memories from childhood, which is good from a qigong perspective because the physical energy of childhood is normally quite healthy. But others have memories from adulthood, such as lounging on a porch swing as they watched the sun set, fishing in a rowboat on a summer afternoon, or relaxing on a park bench watching children play.

When I ask clients to locate a memory, I try to use as few as words as possible, so as not to limit what they look for. "Goodness" is the word I use, which people can define as they wish. At times, clients have used words such as essence, spirit, joy, or "the God within" to describe their experience. The important thing is to find a word and memory that has an energetic resonance for the individual.

When clients have trouble finding a memory that connects them to their inner goodness, there is another, fail-safe way to contact it. To explain it, I share an experience of mine. I was standing in a bakery on a cold, rainy Saturday morning, feeling tired and grumpy after a long work week. There were probably 12 to 15 people in the shop, standing in several lines waiting to purchase bread, cookies and croissants. It should have been a cheery scene, but it was not. Everyone in line looked impatient and tense. No one spoke.

Then, hearing the patter of small feet, I turned to watch a harassed-looking young mother shepherd three small children through the door. She had a baby bundled in her arms and two toddlers in tow. I turned back, resuming my state of self-righteous grumpiness. All of a sudden, a shriek of the purest baby glee pierced the air. Turning with the whole crowd, I saw the baby, now unbundled and still in her mother's arms, glowing with a 1,000-watt smile of delight at the new, wonderfully sweet-smelling environment she'd just encountered. Beauty and goodness shone forth from that baby's face like a bolt of sunshine through a darkened room.

Instantly, the energy of the room was transformed. Virtually everyone began to smile or laugh, helplessly delighted by the baby's delight. The goodness that this tiny creature, so naturally displayed, began to open our own hearts. We began to be kind to one another. If there were any doubt about who was next to be served, people willingly let their neighbor step forward. Many of us began to chat companionably with the person next to us in line.

After sharing that story with a client, I try to convey what I learned from it. I learned that each of us, at some point in our early years of life, had shone with that pure goodness, and that somebody had seen it and taken delight in us. For a moment, or possibly for much longer, our pure and beautiful self had changed someone. I've never had a client not be able to use that story to discover his or her own goodness.

Once a client has found a memory or image, I do a simple meditation exercise with them. I ask them to close their eyes and return to that special moment in time, breathing quietly into the feeling of their goodness and especially being aware of their open heart. It is one of my favorite exercises, as it almost always brings my clients joy. I suggest that they do this meditation at home, as well, because the more one practices it, the easier it is to bring forth the experience of goodness. My clients have found it to be a powerful ally in many situations—as an antidote to shame, as a source of energy to call on during a relationship conflict, or simply as a way to deepen a moment of appreciation.

I believe that my client, Derrick, whom you met in the previous chapter, was able to work through his abuse issues as quickly as he did because he was able to hold onto a sense of his essential goodness. This process can also be powerful for couples. When clients are struggling in relationships, I often suggest that they use this meditation before having an important talk with their partner. Many have reported that the practice helped them to cut through conflict, to speak from their heart about what they needed, and to express what they truly felt for the other person.

The Path to Love, Kindness and Forgiveness

My client, Michelle, was a clinical social worker with her own psychotherapy practice. She had left her marriage three years earlier and had taken a number of steps to help herself heal, including practicing mindfulness meditation. But shortly after her 50th birthday, she came into therapy because, in her words, "Something is missing. I can't really describe it, but there's something I want and I can't find it." She told me she'd chosen me as her therapist because she'd taken a class of mine a few months earlier and had heard me talk about "heart energy." The concept intrigued and attracted her.

Michelle had already gone through two long therapies. During the first, she dealt with the trauma of growing up with an alcoholic, sexually abusive father, and a depressed and distant mother. That therapy lasted six years and had been painful and grueling, but very healing. Her second therapy had lasted almost as long and ultimately helped her to leave her cold, hostile husband. Michelle felt good about all she had done in therapy, but said she was tired of endlessly "wading through my emotions and sorting things out." She wanted something else. Something more.

Because Michelle had heard me talk in class about helping clients find a memory of their goodness, she'd brought with her a photo of herself when she was four years old, standing in front of her seated grandmother. Her beloved "Grammie" had died when Michelle was eight. In the photo, Michelle is wearing a pretty white dress, a bow in her curly blond hair, and a sweet smile. But what made the picture so special to Michelle was not the image of her four-year-old self, but rather the look on her grandmother's face. The delight and love that shone from Grammie's face as she looked at Michelle was almost palpable. "I feel love for me through Grammie's love," she told me.

I saw Michelle maybe 10 times. Our sessions were more meditations than therapy. Sometimes she brought in quiet music; always, she brought in the photo. I didn't have to do much except guide her into her breathing, her body, and her heart. While she could have done that by herself, she was clear that she wanted the presence and support of a man who was very different from her father and husband. She told me, "I want your voice, your kind, loving male voice." As we did the meditations, tears often ran down her face; occasionally, they ran down mine. My task was mainly to stay present and openhearted with Michelle, which she made quite easy to do. I felt like a midwife to someone who had already done the prep work elsewhere and had simply asked me to help her give birth to something beautiful.

Eventually, we talked about how Michelle could bring this heart practice into her own psychotherapy work and into her life at large. She had begun to practice the meditations at home, and as the weeks passed, she began to feel more openhearted. "I am definitely sitting somewhat differently with my clients," she said. "I just feel, well, more loving and compassionate." She smiled, hesitated for a moment, then continued. "But I also just feel kinder to our support staff, my friends, and even the young girl at the dry cleaners." I smiled. But it was what she shared with me in our last session that I remember most vividly.

Michelle came into my office beaming and clearly full of news. Her eyes were so full of love and kindness that it was almost startling. "Patrick, the most amazing thing happened to me last night, you won't believe it," she began. "Or actually, you probably will," she smiled.

"I was practicing my heart meditation at home, and I sank into my heart," she began. "I felt my goodness, felt my love of life, and felt like life loved me. Then, for reasons I can't explain, I decided to visualize my mother and father coming to sit in my living room."

This was a surprise. In the weeks we'd worked together, Michelle had rarely mentioned her parents, who had died several years earlier. She'd told me that she rarely thought about them anymore.

"I really don't know why I did this, having them come and sit with me in my living room," Michelle went on. "But I did, and there they were, seated on my couch. And when I looked at them, especially my father, I felt this love and sadness that I can't explain."

Michelle was quiet for a moment. "You know, I'd never really come to a place of forgiveness of him—I'd just more or less stopped thinking about him. But now I felt something, not really forgiveness, something past that." She hesitated, searching for words. "It seemed like the life he had lived, including what he had done to me, was just so sad for him. What a terrible way to live." Tears rolled down her cheeks.

"I felt sad for him, but I also felt this love for him," she went on, her voice full of wonder. "I wished him well. It was amazing, my heart felt so open. There was nothing standing in the way of my ability to love him. What he had done just wasn't about me."

Michelle looked up at me, her gaze calm. "I don't know if that makes sense, but inside of me it makes so much sense. And now, I just feel free, so free, like I could just skip down the block," she said, laughing. Her happiness was so contagious that I wanted to go skip with her, and in our hearts, I think we did.

What is so exciting about this kind of loving energy is that when we tap into it, we feel care not only for ourselves, but for others as well. When our heart energy is open, we experience that we're not an isolated island, but rather a part of something larger, something that invisibly connects us to other human beings. This sense of community not only helps us to feel cared for, but also to want to extend ourselves to others. I believe that this is what people really come to therapy for. Certainly, they want to let go of their struggles and heal their wounds, but I think that even more fundamentally, people come into therapy yearning for the kind of deep connection we can only experience by both giving and receiving love.

Master Lin often talks about the three pillars of Spring Forest Qigong—Love, Kindness, and Forgiveness. While these are essential and rewarding practices, they can be challenging to realize. Advising someone to "forgive" or "be kinder" is like telling someone to "love yourself more." Nice in theory. But the more a person is able to open his or her heart energy, the easier it is to get in touch with these qualities. When I can help clients open up their heart energy on any consistent basis, I know I'm doing more to help them grow and heal than all the insight in the world. Insight can be useful, and sometimes even life-changing, but I can think of no work more rewarding, or more transformative, than helping someone learn to walk in the world with an open heart.

The Heart of the Therapist

As I've noted earlier, it's vitally important for therapists to practice breathing and visualization if they want to teach these practices to others. It's no less important for therapists who want to help open a client's heart energy to also work on opening their own heart. We therapists are not trained to be openhearted with our clients. We are trained to be caring, but clinical, taking care not to love our clients because of the potential to harm them by confounding their therapeutic process or exploiting their vulnerability. This kind of response to a client, which is driven more by hunger than by love, is not what I'm talking about here.

Sitting in a session with an open heart and letting your loving energy flow freely isn't about hunger. Nor is it even about feeling benevolent toward a suffering client. It is about your goodness seeing their goodness, your humanity witnessing their humanity. These days, when some difficult or confusing moment arises in a therapy session and I ask myself what to do next, the answer that often comes to me is simply, "Patrick, open your heart." It changes everything.

One of the great benefits of learning qigong, at least the way you're taught in Master Lin classes, is that you can practice it any time, wherever you are. (Master Lin teaches that you can even learn to turn your sleep into a meditation, thereby practicing qigong 24 hours a day!) The results—I now rarely end a day feeling tired, and I virtually never feel spent. The reason is that all day long I am cultivating energy, drawing energy from the universe and keeping myself replenished and balanced. As I sit with clients all day, I frequently use breathing and visualization to keep my mind quiet, my body relaxed, and myself in balance. Those benefits are wonderful, but it gets even better.

Through my work, I get to work on cultivating an open heart all day long. In essence, my psychology practice is a meditation practice. With every client, I work on being openhearted and loving, fostering an energy unlike anything I'd been taught in graduate school or in any training program. This is not some generic, "love for all people" kind of response. It is very particular to the client, and the more I get to know that person, the more my heart energy opens specifically to them. In the last two years, I've had more clients spontaneously tell me that they know I love them then I had in the previous 20 years. This loving energy knows the limits of what I can do, and the boundaries that are necessary. But that energy also wants the best for my client, and trusts in the power of that caring for healing and transformation.

I am currently working with Roy, a charming, fast-talking, compulsive gambler who loves to argue with just about anyone. When he came in last week, he told me in quite provocative terms about a short, but nasty, interchange he'd had with his wife. He had told her to change her clothes before they went out to a party because she looked "like a stuffed turkey" in the outfit she had on. When she expressed her outrage, he followed up with, "You've put on 20 pounds and none of them are pretty." She hasn't spoken to him since.

Roy reported the interaction to me in a way that sounded like a belligerent schoolyard challenge, the kind of tone that communicated, "That's what I said to her and what are you going to do about it?" Given that I'm a guy, a former Marine and a black belt in Tae Kwon Do, I almost bit. My first, internal response was to demand, "Well, did you apologize?" in a challenging, condemning tone. But just in time, I stopped, took a breath, and focused on sinking my energy into my heart. I immediately saw past the tough, provocative exterior of Roy to the man who so much wanted to stop being a jerk and be more connected to others, especially his wife. Gently, I asked, "Were you able to apologize?" The words were nearly the same but my tone, now, was one of invitation and acceptance.

Roy let out a long breath. Then he stared down at the floor and muttered, "I'm too ashamed of myself to apologize." Looking up at me, he said, "I know I shouldn't say stuff like that. We've talked about it, for Christ's sake, how many times? But I just can't stop it from coming out, and then I can't stand myself for not being able to stop it. So, at that moment, I'm not even really thinking about my wife, but about what a loser I am. I guess that's a little self-centered, isn't it?" he said with a weak smile. I asked Roy to take a breath and just look at both himself and his wife with compassion. As he closed his eyes and began to breathe deeply, I saw his face grow long with sadness. We then began to work with his sorrow about the ways he has hurt and distanced the woman he loved.

When My Heart is a Block of Wood

On certain days, being openhearted and grounded in my body and breath is not just difficult, but seemingly impossible. It is a mystery to me why on some days I can, and on other days I can't, find that openhearted place. I may be caught up in the vagaries of my life, or I may be feeling tired and lazy, or for some unknown reason I'm just unable to feel loving toward my clients. When I asked Master Lin what I should do on days like that, he told me to visualize and sense a lotus flower, or the early-morning summer sun, in the heart of the person I'm with. Both of these natural phenomena are powerful healing images in qigong.

A few months ago, I was sitting with a man who had been my client for almost five years. David was living in a stale, empty and lifeless marriage. He was trying to bring it to an end—actually he'd been trying to for a couple of years—but he was so emotionally blocked that he couldn't move. Every time he got close to experiencing some grief or anger, he would freeze up and dissociate from his body. It happened like clockwork.

On this bright autumn afternoon, David was talking about another week in which his wife had been very depressed and unwilling to do anything for herself or for the marriage. Because he had grown up with a lot of emotional deprivation, it was hard for David to muster any belief that he deserved more in life. He knew that his marriage was unlikely to change, and also that he was very afraid to be alone. Living with a depressed wife who had no interest in him gave him the illusion of companionship, if not the reality.

As David talked and got closer to feeling his grief, we both knew what was going to happen. He was going to shut down. I wasn't feeling very heart-centered this day, and found myself thinking, "Can't he just get on with it?" Then I thought of my conversation with Master Lin. I began to visualize a lotus flower, a beautiful white blossom sitting in David's heart. I tried to imagine and sense its texture, its dimensions, and even its subtle fragrance. As David continued to talk, I just sat with him and focused on the lotus flower. I began to experience that this flower was the goodness in David's heart. As this awareness expanded, so did my heart.

I'm not sure how long I sat like this with David – 3 or 4 minutes would be my guess. He talked on, and just as his eyes began to fill with tears, he blinked them back and totally shut down. Sitting with this man whom I cared about deeply, seeing him stuck once again and sensing the goodness in his heart, I didn't try to do anything. I just said to him, "David, I just wish there was something I could do for you right here, right now."

He looked at me with a strange expression on his face. Then he said something that surprised us both. "I think I need to know if you love me."

I smiled—a loving smile, I think—and said, "I sure do."

He put his head down and wept for two minutes.

David is still struggling to end his marriage. That day, though, opened a door that he has since walked through several times – a door to grief about his lifelong loneliness. He talks occasionally, usually very tentatively, about our relationship and about knowing that I love him. I believe that what changed that day had little to do with my long-honed, traditional therapeutic skills. What happened was that I allowed myself to see my client's essential goodness—beyond all talk or behavior or history—and my reluctant heart cracked open.[3]

Keep it Simple

As I've emphasized throughout the book, the process of healing is much simpler than we've been led to believe. Whenever you experience some kind of emotional or psychological difficulty, start by doing some conscious breathing. (*Refer back to Chapter 1 for a refresher on this process.*) Are you experiencing some kind of inner conflict? Close your eyes and breathe. Are you feeling anxious or depressed? Breathe. A relationship problem? Breathe. You cannot go wrong with breathing: It is the very foundation of healing and health.

Once you begin to experience some inner calm via breathing, you can "change the channel" on your negative thinking by imagining something positive. (*Refer back to Chapter 3 for a primer on creating healing imagery.*) If you're embroiled in a conflict with your partner, for example, imagine him or her doing something kind for you. If you're working on a task and find yourself stuck, imagine plunging into the project and thoroughly enjoying it the way you threw yourself into finger-painting or building block towers when you were a small child. You'll know the imagery is bearing fruit when you feel the energy change in your body. Once you learn how to do this, you can begin to shift your energy in just one breath and one visualization.

Speaking of energy, remember, you can powerfully affect your energy by small changes you make in your daily life. So put on some music that makes your body smile. Put that brownie away and eat some broccoli salad! Take a walk or a run. Watch something on TV that actually engages your mind and soul.

When you sit at the dinner table at home or hang out at the coffee machine at work, try to look at the people around you with your heart rather than your head. Sink into your body and imagine their essential goodness—visualize a flower or a ray of sunshine beaming from their heart to yours. When you learn to open your heart, it becomes a way to navigate life, reliably steering you where you need to go. It will tell you who to be with and who to leave, and you will know how to do both with care and integrity. The more you practice openheartedness, the more it will become second nature to you.

Meanwhile, the next time you find yourself feeling stressed out, look at yourself in the mirror and do an intervention so your friends won't have to. You might say, "Okay Self, right now I am compromising my immune system. There is less blood than there should be flowing to my organs, brain and extremities. I am not processing my food efficiently, and I am probably putting undue stress on my heart."

"Furthermore, Self, there is a good chance that I'm creating some anxiety or depression that is interfering with my well-being, both emotional and physical. Who needs it? So, Self, aside from sinking into my body and breathing, visualizing inner peace and health, making my living environment more energetically peaceful, and using my consciousness to live from my heart, what do I need to change in my life?"

Listen for the answer. It will come. Once it does, you can choose to act. It's that simple. And, as Master Lin often says in parting, "Now have a good and lucky day."

INTO THE HEART
AND INTO THE WORLD

This exercise brings it all together. If you take a few minutes to learn this simple practice, and if you're willing to work with it regularly, it can fundamentally change the way you interact with the world around you.

First, you need to retrieve a memory. Find a memory of a time when you were aware of your own goodness, a time when you knew that something inside you was pure, beautiful and belonged to you without your having to do anything about it. Or imagine someone looking at you, probably as an infant, and feeling awe or joy as they saw your goodness shine forth from your eyes and smile, the goodness that was innately yours, and that was so beautiful to behold. Close your eyes and use your heart to look back over your life and find that moment. If you have read the last chapter, you probably have a good idea of how to approach this process.

You will know you have found this memory by what it does to your heart. Many of my clients have described a feeling of "openness," a "tingling," or "a sense of goodwill toward all things." Many also say that when they contact this sense of goodness, they experience that it has always been in them, and that it always will be. What is so powerful about this practice is that many people have been so hurt and damaged by past experiences that they have been utterly unaware of their innate goodness. But it's there. Sometimes it can be challenging to find, but if we take sufficient time to look, it will show itself to us. Nobody can tarnish it, diminish it, or take it away. It belongs to us.

Whether you have retrieved an actual memory, or have imagined someone else witnessing and being moved by your essential goodness, you're ready for the next step. Find a quiet, comfortable place where you won't be interrupted. If you like, put on some peaceful music. Then sit down and close your eyes. Let yourself really sink into your breath, into your body, and into that memory or image of your essential goodness. Let your consciousness of that memory, or image, sink into your heart area.

Notice what this practice does to your heart, energetically. Do you feel it open up, become a bit more expansive? Become aware of what it does to your face—does it feel a little softer, looser? What is your overall sense of emotional well-being? The deeper you sink into this experience and allow yourself to feel this heart-opening energy, the more deeply it will affect you. "The more powerful the image, the more powerful the energy" is something we hear a lot in qigong. So let yourself fully be with your image, and linger there. Breathe, relax, and be conscious of this experience with your whole energetic being.

Of course, the more frequently you do this exercise, the more powerful the experience will become. Also, the more you do it, the easier it will become to recall this state of being at other times—when you're with your kids, your lover, your accountant, or the tired and hostile person at the gas station cash register. You cannot help but walk down the road of life with a springier step when your heart is open. Nor can you stay too focused on yourself. The heart is not built for self-absorption; it inherently looks for, and into, the hearts of others. So, for your sake, and for the world's, sink onto your heart and let it guide you.

BIBLIOGRAPHY

Introduction

1 Lin, C., <u>Spring Forest Qigong: Level I for Health</u> (Mpls., MN., Spring Forest Publishing, 1999), p. 18.

2 See www.springforestqigong.com, on left side of page click on research for study of SFQ and depression.

3 Shih, T.K., <u>Qigong Therapy</u> (Barrytown, N.Y., Station Hill Press, 1994), p. 57.

4 See Cohen's website at http://www.qigonghealing.com/qigong/benefits.html.

Chapter 1: The Power of the Breath

1 Cohen, K.S., <u>Ken Cohen's Guide to Healthy Breathing</u> (CD) (Boulder, CO., Soundstrue.com. 1996).

2 Ibid.

3 Benson, H, <u>Timeless Healing: The Power and Biology of Belief</u> (New York, Fireside, 1996,) pp. 146 - 148.

4 Weil, A, <u>Breathing: The Master Key to Self Healing</u> (CD) (Boulder, CO., Soundstrue.com, 1999).

5 Ibid.

6 Lewis, D. <u>The Tao of Natural Breathing</u> (Berkeley, CA., Rodmell Press, 2006) p. 42.

7 See www.attentionspan.net/breathing.html.

8 Weil, Ibid.

9 Lewis, Ibid. p. 15.

Exercise 1

1 Olson, S.A., <u>Translator, The Jade Emperor's Mind Seal Classic: A Taoist Guide to Health, Longevity and Immortality</u>. (St.Paul, MN. Dragon Door Publications, 1992), p. 70.

2 Ibid, Lewis, <u>Free Your Breath, Free Your Life.</u>, p. 14.

Chapter 2: Stress: The Hidden Saboteur

1 Pine, R. trans., <u>Taoteching</u> (San Francisco, CA, Mercury House, 1996). p. 48.

2 See Sapolsky, R.M. <u>Why Zebras Don't Get Ulcers</u> (New York, W.H. Freeman and Company, 1998).

3 Cohen, K.S. <u>The Way of Qigong: The Art and Science of Chinese Energy Healing</u> (New York, Random House, 1997) p. 11.

4 See www.nichd.nih.gov/news/releases/stress.cfm.

Chapter 3: The Mind's Eye: Using Imagery to Heal

1 See http:mail.med.upenn.edu/~abeck.

2 <u>NY Times</u>, D. Goleman, August 17, 1993.

3 Naparstek, B. <u>Invisible Heroes: Survivors of Trauma and How They Heal.</u> (New York, Bantam Books, 2004) p. 149.

4 Ibid. p. 140.

5 See Sykes Wylie, M, " Mindsight" <u>Family Therapy Networker</u>, Vol 25 #5, (Sept/Oct 2004).

Exercise 2

1 Ibid. Olson, p. 70.

Chapter 4: Energy: An Invisible Force for Healing

1 Lin, <u>Spring Forest Qigong: Level I for Health</u>, p. 8.

2 Lin, C, & Rebstock, G., <u>Born A Healer</u> (Mpls., MN, Spring Forest Publishing, 2002), p. 56.

3 See Ch. 1, Watts, A., <u>Taoism: Way beyond Seeking</u> (Boston, Turtle Publishing, 1997).

Chapter 5: Coming Home To The Self: A Taoist Framework

1 See introduction, Cleary, T., Vitality, <u>Energy, Spirit: A Taoist Sourcebook</u>. (Boston, MA. Shambhala, 1991).

2 See Ch. 12, Wong, E., <u>Cultivating Stillness: A Taoist Manual for Transforming Body and Mind</u>. (Boston, Shambhala, 1992).

3 See Ch. 4, Watts, <u>Taoism</u>.

4 Watts, A., <u>Tao: The Watercourse Way</u>. (New York, Pantheon, 1975). pp. 75 - 77.

5 Blofeld, J., <u>Taoism: The Road to Immortality</u>. (Boston, Shambahla, 1985). pp. 9 - 10.

Chapter 6: Beyond Words: Psychotherapy with the Mind, Body and Heart

1 Johanson, G., & Kurtz, R., <u>Grace Unfolding: Psychotherapy in the Spirit of the Taoteching</u>. (New York, Bell Tower, New York. 199), p1.

2 Lewis, <u>The Tao of Natural Breathing</u>, p. 47.

3 Ibid. Johanson & Kurtz, p. 12.

Chapter 7: Anything But *That!* Working with the Resistance to Change

1 Levine, P. <u>Walking the Tiger: Healing Trauma</u>. (Berkeley, North Atlantic 1997), p. 82.

Chapter 8: Healing Trauma

1 Naparstek, <u>Invisible Heroes</u>, p. 15.

2 Levine, <u>Walking the Tiger</u>, p. 34.

3 Johnson, D.H. & Grand I. J., Ed. <u>The Body in Psychotherapy: Inquiries in Somatic Psychology</u>. (Berkeley, CA., North Atlantic Books 1998), p. 22.

4 Ibid. Naparstek., p. 161.

5 Johanson & Kurtz, <u>Grace Unfolding</u>, p. 29.

Chapter 9: A Heart-Centered Life

1 Ibid, Olson, p. 60.

2 Lin, C. <u>Self Concentration Meditation</u>

3 Dougherty, P., "Breathing Lessons", <u>Psychotherapy Networker</u>, Vol 30, #3, May/June 06.

About the Author

Patrick Dougherty, M.A., L.P. is a Licensed Psychologist, who has been a practicing psychotherapist in St. Paul, MN since 1977. He has been teaching psychotherapists how to incorporate Qigong into psychotherapy since 2000, with continuing education credits approved by the MN Board of Social Work in 2002 and the MN Boards of Psychology, and Marriage and Family Therapy in 2004.

For more information,

contact Patrick Dougherty at www.theheartembodied.com

26795616R00113

Made in the USA
San Bernardino, CA
22 February 2019